KT-493-216

ZEN SEEDS
Reflections of a Female Priest

by Shundo Aoyama

translated by
Patricia Daien Bennage

Kosei Publishing Co.   *Tokyo*

294.3

Reproduced on the front cover is a portion of *Haboku San-sui-ga* (Landscape in *Haboku* Style), a hanging scroll executed in ink on paper by the Zen priest Sesshu in 1495 and designated a National Treasure by the Japanese government. Photo courtesy of the Tokyo National Museum.

This book was originally published in Japanese under the title *Utsukushiki Hito Ni*.

Editing by Margaret E. Taylor. Book design and typography by Morio Takanashi. Cover design by Hiroyuki Araki. This book is set in a computer version of Baskerville with a computer version of Optima for display.

First English edition, 1990

Published by Kōsei Publishing Co., Kōsei Building, 2-7-1 Wada, Suginami-ku, Tokyo 166, Japan. Copyright © 1983 by Shundō Aoyama, 1990 by Kōsei Publishing Co.; all rights reserved. Printed in Japan.

ISBN 4-333-01478-6   LCC Card No. applied for

200023893

Contents

Editorial Note

In this book the names of all pre-modern Japanese are given in the Japanese style, with the surname first, and those of all modern (post-1868) Japanese are given in the Western style, with the surname last.

Hearing the Voice of the Valley Stream

The water of the valley stream is always flowing. It races on, not pausing for even an instant. Its sound, to me, is the sound of time.

The water of time glistens on the riverbed of the universe. Though theirs is a much slower flow, stones, trees, houses, and towns are flowing too. Human beings and all things that have life flow. Thought and culture, too, flow. That all these appear to be unchanging is but illusion.

We make every effort to keep things as they are, because human beings, alone, lament transience. Yet no matter how we grieve or protest, there is no way to impede the flow of anything. If we but see things as they are and flow with them, we may find enjoyment in transience. Because human life is transient, all manner of figures are woven into its fabric.

At the beginning of zazen meditation, when all is still, the sound of the valley stream is loud and clear. When we pace slowly after meditation, to ease leg pains and drowsiness, the sound of the stream seems to be less audible. When zazen is completed, the sound cannot be heard at all. Why should this be?

The sound of the valley stream does not actually increase, diminish, or disappear. When the waves in our minds become calm, we can hear the voices of the water, pebbles, grasses and trees, rivers, and mountains teaching us. When our thoughts are occupied with events in the outer world, these nonsentient beings cease their speech. Rather, it is not that they no longer speak but that when we are caught up by the outer world we have no ears to hear.

As it is with our ears, so it is with our eyes. When the mind's eye is clear, we see all existences naturally, as they are; but the moment our attention is distracted by even a single thought of the outer world, that which is seen is no longer registered truthfully in our minds. We become blind, just as we become deaf to the sounds around us. When our attention is pulled here and there, we no longer see what we should be seeing, hear what we should be hearing.

When we listen subconsciously to the sound of flowing water, does it not seem to create a rhythm? Yet not a single drop of water passes over the same rock twice, and the murmur of water rushing over a rock is constantly changing. Sameness is but an illusion of the human ears, eyes, mind. Water that has once flowed along a riverbed can never retrace its course. Human life is no different. It is only our mundane eyes and minds that see yesterday as being the same as today.

Enlightened eyes and minds should recognize that each moment has a form different from that of any other moment.

I Want to Become a Beautiful Person

People walk about totally unaware that their faces and bodies reveal everything about the way they have lived. Such nakedness can be embarrassing, even frightening.

All we have thought or said and all we have done since birth have molded our faces, bodies, and personalities. With a single glance, a clear-eyed person can perceive our entire history.

Was it Lincoln who said that a man is responsible for his looks after the age of forty? It is in the forties that the face and body, as if shaped continuously from birth by an unseen chisel, reveal a beauty or ugliness that cannot be disguised by cosmetics or clothing.

The modern Japanese poet and calligrapher Yaichi Aizu once wrote to an acquaintance, "My friend, by being circumspect in everything I think and do, by having a heart at peace, I hope to become a beautiful person." I feel that I, too, would like to age in that way.

A Heavenly Wind

I pause in my gardening to look at a small bird overhead whose cry has broken the silence. A refreshing wind sweeping down from the Japan Alps dries the sweat on my brow. Joy in life, joy in work wells up in me.

"The wind is cold today, isn't it?" comments an elderly woman passing by.

"Whose house cannot give a welcome to the bright moon, the refreshing breeze?" asks the *Hekigan-roku* (Blue Cliff Records). The bright moon shines into every house; every house lies in the path of the refreshing breeze. Does one feel the breeze as refreshing or as a heartlessly cold wind? The difference lies not in the wind but in the person perceiving it. Someone once told me that such a breeze is called a "heavenly wind."

Centuries ago, when Chao-chou asked Zen Master Nan-ch'üan if he should seek the Way, Nan-ch'üan answered, "If you try for it, you will become separated from it."

That which we call paradise or happiness or the Dharma or enlightenment cannot be sought outside us. It will be found only when we notice that we are innately endowed with it.

If It Sloshes, There Isn't Enough

Having been invited to a tea ceremony, I entered a room in a nearby temple, where I noticed a hanging scroll in the tokonoma alcove. The scroll, a painting of a drinking gourd, carried the following inscription by the modern Zen Master Rosen Takashina: "If it sloshes, there isn't enough." What wit lies behind that remark.

A gourd filled to the brim with wine makes no sound when shaken. If there is only a little wine left in the bottom of a gourd, it sloshes. People are like gourds. Human beings who are truly self-aware remain calm and unruffled no matter what happens. When people rush around busily, complaining and making excuses, they prove their lack of wisdom.

The same thought occurred to me once when I was traveling down a valley stream in a small boat. Upstream, where the water is shallow, its surface is choppy and it flows noisily. Downstream, where the stream is swollen and the water deep, its surface is smooth and calm and it flows silently.

The words on that scroll come to mind whenever I feel inclined to fuss about something.

The Horsefly

Once, as I was counseling a sobbing woman who had announced that she wanted to die, a horsefly flew into my room. In trying to escape the room, the horsefly repeatedly drove itself against the window, fell to the floor stunned, got up, and again attacked the same spot on the window. That made me think of the early-nineteenth-century Zen

Master Fugai, and I told the woman this story.

A prosperous man who had called on Zen Master Fugai in his dilapidated temple in Osaka was complaining of his problems. Just then a horsefly flew into the room. It began diving at the window again and again. Fugai watched the horsefly intently, apparently not listening to his visitor.

The impatient man of wealth said with heavy irony, "You seem to be very fond of horseflies."

To this, Fugai replied, "I'm sorry. It's just that all this is a great pity for the poor horsefly. This temple is known for its state of disrepair. Despite the fact that it is free to fly out through a hole almost anywhere, this horsefly keeps flinging itself against a single spot, convinced that that's the only possible exit. If it keeps this up, it will die. But it is not only the horsefly that is to be pitied."

Loving

I once presented an acquaintance with a souvenir I had chosen with care during a trip, expecting her to be delighted with it. She surprised me by saying, "I don't actually want this myself, but I'll take it because it will make a nice gift for someone." I blurted out, "If I'd known you would want to give it away, I wouldn't have given it to you in the first place."

In that instant, I realized my error. I saw how dreadful it is to mentally hold on to something I have already given away. I was unable to give unconditionally, saying, "You are free to throw it out or give it away. It is enough that you have accepted it."

I felt grateful, thinking, "How fortunate I am to have been exposed to the teachings of the Buddha, so that I could recognize that part of me that clings to possessions." To paraphrase Rabindranath Tagore, "May my loving you not become a burden to you, for I have freely chosen to love you."

In loving and giving unconditionally, Tagore avoided burdening the person he addressed. Realizing how much my thinking differed from Tagore's, I blushed in shame.

In Another's Place

An elderly woman who had told me that nothing made her happier than coming to the temple regularly to sing in the Buddhist chorus was absent one day. The next time the group gathered to rehearse, I asked her what had happened.

"Well, I got ready and I reached the door just as a visitor arrived. She asked if I was on my way out. If I had said yes, she would have turned around and gone home. Thinking that would be a pity, since she had taken the trouble to come, I said, 'No, your timing is very good. I've just now returned. Do, please, come in.' So she came in, and I wasn't able to come to rehearsal."

If that had happened to me, what would I have

said? "I'm so sorry you've taken the trouble to come, because I'm just on my way out" or "I'm just on my way out, but it doesn't matter if I'm a little bit late, so please come in" or some other equally self-centered greeting. The old woman was an inspiration to me for her tact and thoughtfulness.

We Are All Related

I would like to tell you a story about the seventeenth-century Zen Master Bankei, who had no use for the koans traditional to Zen.

One day a woman came to Zen Master Bankei to complain about her daughter-in-law. "Hmmm. Is that so? You don't say," responded Bankei, absorbing the woman's complaints as a blotter does ink. When she had finished, he said just this: "Long ago you yourself were a daughter-in-law. Weren't you once like your daughter-in-law? Don't think of her as someone apart from you. Hers is the path you once walked. Her life is an extension of yours into the past." Since Bankei had listened to all her complaints and her spirits were restored, these words satisfied the woman.

Sometime afterward the daughter-in-law came to Zen Master Bankei to complain about her mother-in-law. Having listened patiently to the complaints, Bankei said, "Someday you yourself will be a mother-in-law. Don't think of your mother-in-law as someone apart from you. Hers is

the path you will take one day. Her life is an extension of yours into the future. If you think of your
life in this way, it's hard to complain about it, isn't
it?'' As with the mother-in-law, Bankei's words
set the daughter-in-law's heart at ease.

When we realize that we all share a single life—
as brothers, sisters, parents, children—we can put
ourselves in the position of any other person we
know.

Zen Master Dogen, who founded the Soto Zen
sect in the thirteenth century, had a broad vision
of this concept of a shared life that even encompassed objects. In his *Tenzo Kyokun* (Instructions to
the Kitchen Supervisor), Dogen quotes an old saying, ''See the pot as your own head; see the water
as your life,'' and also says, ''Use the property
and possessions of the community as carefully as if
they were your own eyes.'' Everything is alive in
the vast ocean of the Dharma world.

Reflecting on how I live my own life as a student
of the Buddha's teachings, I realize that I cannot
measure up to these examples no matter how hard
I try. All I can see is my own self-centeredness.
Yet had I not been exposed to the teachings of the
Buddha, I probably wouldn't have been able to
see even that much.

Selfless Religious Practice

They say in Zen temples, ''When the wooden
block is struck, it's the dining hall; when the

bell sounds, it's the sutra hall," for the monks are called to meals by the striking of a wooden block and to sutra chanting by a bell. Everything we do in Zen is announced not through words but through the sounding of instruments. When an instrument is sounded, practitioners must obey its signal at once. No matter what task one is performing, the signal must be obeyed instantly, even if it means leaving one's work half done.

Though this seems an easy rule to follow, it is actually quite difficult. "If I work just a little longer, I can finish everything" or "Just a little longer; this isn't a good place to stop" or some other excuse for not obeying is offered. It is at such times that we are caught up in self-centered thoughts of our own affairs, our own judgment. I tell practitioners, "The signals are a supreme command. When you are called to cross the river of death, will you be able to say, 'Please wait a moment'? You must follow instructions selflessly and answer yes without hesitating. This is the most important attitude."

To paraphrase Zen Master Dogen, "Even if you practice zazen so earnestly that you break through the floor, if your practice is only for yourself it will come to nothing."

Monks Make Excellent Friends

The Buddha said, "Having excellent friends and

keeping good company is not half the sacred Way; it is the very Way itself.''

In the *Shobo-genzo Zuimonki,* a collection of discourses, Zen Master Dogen explained the importance of excellent friends: ''Even students of Zen who are weak-willed in seeking the Way should associate with good practitioners and learn from them whenever possible. No matter how difficult or painful the training may be, students should seek their guidance.'' Dogen's warm concern for and empathy with lay believers are apparent in this expansion of the Buddha's comment.

One Japanese word for monk or the monkhood is derived from the Sanskrit word *sangha,* meaning ''group'' or ''union.'' One person alone cannot form a sangha, or community of believers. Well aware of human weakness, the Buddha cautioned against solitary practice. Alone, it is hard to practice zazen for even an hour. But if one is part of a group, an intensive zazen retreat of three or seven days or a monastic life of many years is possible.

Zazen is not a form of competition. Even though we may think we can practice in isolation, we cannot. As Dogen pointed out, ''People should help each other by combining their strengths as they practice religious discipline.'' It is because we derive such strength from the group that we are able to persevere in our religious practice. That is why monks make excellent friends.

Revering him as the teacher who awakened to the true Way, and with his teachings as our guide, we practice the Buddha's Way at all times in our daily lives, supported by friends who aspire to the same Way. If we are ill, so be it; if we are poor, so be it. In the very midst of sickness and poverty we practice the Way, relying on the Three Treasures—the Buddha, his teachings (the Dharma), and the community of Buddhist believers (the Sangha).

Can any happiness surpass that afforded by this way of life?

Follow the Flow of the Stream

Zen Master Ta-mei Fa-ch'ang lived in China during the late eighth and early ninth centuries. After religious training under his master Ma-tsu Tao-i, he secluded himself deep in the mountains. He made himself a robe from the giant lotus leaves that grew abundantly in the marsh, and lived on the seeds of the pine trees. In this way, he persevered in his zazen practice for over thirty years.

A priest once strayed from the mountain path and by chance came upon Ta-mei's grass hut. When he asked for the path leading to the village, Ta-mei replied, "Follow the flow of the stream," which means that, if you simply follow the stream, you will find your way out of the mountains.

An essayist, Wariko Kai, wrote this poem:

Although there are rocks and tree roots,

Rippling along, just rippling along,
The water runs.

If our ordinary, self-centered viewpoint is domi-
nant, rocks and tree roots are undesirable. But if
we change our point of view, then the very fact
that there are rocks and tree roots makes the valley
stream more beautiful and the sight of waves break-
ing upon them beyond description.

When we perceive joy, anger, happiness, and
sorrow as enriching our lives, just as rocks and
tree roots and water spray embellish nature, then
we are able to accept whatever happens and live
like flowing water, without clinging to anything.

Appetite Is Also a Blessing

At the end of a zazen gathering that is held at my
temple each summer, as I was seeing off Zen
Master Kosho Uchiyama in our car en route to the
station, a nun sitting beside the driver exclaimed,
"Oh, the apples are beginning to turn red!" and
"The tomatoes look so good!"

Zen Master Uchiyama, listening from the back
seat, smiled and murmured, "No matter what
food you are blessed with, if you weren't blessed
with an appetite too, you'd be in a bad way,
wouldn't you?"

I was taken aback by this. I had taken it for
granted that I would always have an appetite and

could eat at any time. So appetite was a blessing, too! Come to think of it, all sorts of treats can be lined up at the bedside of someone seriously ill with the idea that eating will make him better. But no matter how that person is urged to eat, without the fundamental element of appetite, he may not be able to consume even a single grain of rice. On the other hand, with a good appetite, we can be sustained by thin rice gruel and sesame salt.

Whether or not the availability of food is a problem, we must not forget the joy of having an appetite.

Plum Blossoms Open the Early Spring

When we talk about paradise or happiness, what generally comes to mind? First of all, we might think that money brings happiness. If only we had money, all of our difficulties would be solved. Money, money, money, all our life we chase after money. I wonder how many people end their lives having been slaves to money? Will we really be happy if we have money? I think not. Tragedies may even occur because of money.

Goethe said that the amount of money indispensable to a human being is not really that much, and he concluded that it is part of human nature to long for money. The same is true for fame. If we equate the satisfaction of these ever-escalating desires for money and fame with happiness, we will never find true happiness anywhere.

Everyone desires to be rich rather than poor. Everyone wishes to be healthy rather than ill. Everyone wants to be a success rather than a failure. No matter how hard you work during your lifetime, there may be times when you have to go without food for the day. No matter how much you complain of illness, you have to be ill when the time comes. Even if it is an illness you will die from, you cannot escape it. No matter how much confidence or capability you have, there may be failures.

Happiness that depends on what you acquire or become is only conditional happiness, not true happiness. No matter what happens, it is all right. If you become ill, then just be ill; if you are poor, then just be poor. Unless you accept your present circumstances, happiness cannot be attained. To face any situation and accept it with open arms if it cannot be avoided molds the attitude enabling you to see that such a wonderful way of living is possible. This is indeed something of consequence. As soon as this attitude is achieved, you have reached paradise, anytime, anywhere, and in any circumstances.

Zen Master Dogen's teacher, Ju-ching, said, "Plum blossoms open the early spring," not "Plum blossoms open in early spring." It is the plum blossoms that bring the spring. Once this idea is accepted, spring must be everywhere.

Everyone Is in the Palm of the Buddha's Hand

Whether we are aware of it or not, whether we be sinners or saints, we are all living in the palm of the Buddha's hand. Whether the Buddha is denied or praised, the Buddha watches over us all, embracing us unconditionally.

In the classic Chinese novel *Monkey,* the magically gifted monkey flies to what he thinks is the end of the universe. But still he was not able to leave the palm of the Buddha.

No evil can drive one from the palm of the Buddha. This is what Shinran, founder of the True Pure Land sect, said: "There is no evil that can obstruct the working of the original vow of Amida Buddha [to save all sentient beings]." We think that if we do something bad, we will be punished for it; or we think that benefits depend on the amount of our offerings. Such miserly calculations by human beings are, needless to say, not indicative of the true Buddha.

"Even though it be the same water, when a cow drinks it, it becomes milk. When a snake drinks it, it becomes poison." I believe these words are from the Nirvana Sutra. Imbibing the same water brings benefit to some people, while it poisons others. Originally it was the same substance. We should not forget this. Cows and poisonous snakes are not distinct beings, nor are they distinct from ourselves. This is the ultimate basis of all manifestations. We have all received the same gift of life from the Buddha. By the venerable strength of the Buddha, we live or die, go or stay, sit or lie down, all the while experiencing joys and sorrows. Unaware of that truth, we separate the self from the great life-force of the universe and place it in the center. Then, thinking and acting according to personal gain and loss, or likes and dislikes, we become like poisonous snakes. When instead we are aware of the gift of life from the Buddha and the frame around the self is removed, we become beneficial like cows.

In his *Shobo-genzo* (The Treasury of the True Dharma Eye), Zen Master Dogen says, "To study the Way is to study the self. To study the self is to forget the self. To forget the self is to be enlightened by all things. To be enlightened by all things is to remove the barriers between oneself and others."

Four Ways of Seeing Water

A fourth grader in elementary school wrote this poem, "The Playground":

> When playing in the schoolyard,
> We say, "It's so little; it's so little."
> When made to gather stones for morning assembly,
> We say, "It's so huge; it's so huge."

This child noticed and was able to vividly convey the feelings of ordinary human beings. When we are completely absorbed in the enjoyment of the things we like to do, ten hours may seem like less than an hour. But when we have to do something we dislike, an hour may seem like a day. The poem describes how elusive the standard is by which ordinary human beings measure what they see and think.

A number of years ago in summer, I was hospitalized for twenty days. Following abdominal surgery, I had absolutely no appetite for five days. At first I was offered juice, milk, or gruel. If I do not eat a little, I will not recuperate, I thought, so I gathered up my courage and took a sip of milk, but for the rest of the day that tiny sip of milk seemed to stick in my throat. Meanwhile, two or three bottles of milk accumulated at my bedside.

At this point a good friend visited me. Wiping perspiration from her face, she noted the bottles of milk I had been unable to drink. Making great gulping sounds, she polished off two of the bottles. I felt as though I were observing some strange spectacle. I had made such an effort to take one sip, and even that had stayed in my throat all day, but my friend easily finished two whole bottles. Could she be all right? This thought fleetingly crossed my mind.

The following day another friend brought loquats, peeled them, cut them in little pieces, and put a piece in my mouth. It was tasteless; I felt like I was chewing sand. That one bite was enough. What I had left uneaten, my friend finished with great relish and went home. When three or four more days continued like this, I came to feel that there was nothing delicious in the whole world.

On another day a friend came with some home-made pudding. Since she had gone to all this trouble, I thought I had better have some and took a spoonful. But just as I expected, it was like eating garbage. Again, I could only shake my head. Just as I was looking on with incomprehension as my friend ate the remaining pudding with great gusto, it came to me: I'm sick! This should have been obvious, but to me it was a great discovery.

That is the way it goes in the world, I said to myself. If we could only notice that we are ailing, there would be no problem; and moreover, my awareness of being ill comes not from my own strength, but from the strength of the Buddha.

After my friend had gone, I tried to analyze this precious experience again, alone in my quiet room. I thought: I have no appetite. Everything I eat is awful, really awful. If what I am eating at present is so awful, what my friend eats has to be awful, too. I am not convinced by the hearty way she eats. In short, I measure other people by the standard of my own experience. If they deviate from it, I am likely to blame them for being mistaken.

It is natural that, since people lead different lives, they have many ways of seeing things. Each of them, thinking the way he or she sees things is absolutely right, measures other people by that standard and always judges the other party to be mistaken. This is where I fall short of enlightenment, and it is also the key to understanding the mundane world. How I feel, see things, and think at the present moment depends on the limited experiences and knowledge accumulated in my past life, my present health, and my emotional ups and downs. That is a tentative interpretation or judgment, but never an absolute one. If I am aware of this basic element of human nature in the ordinary person or in the sick person within myself, no troubles or discord will take place in my life or in the world around me. Moreover, I shall never forget that what clearly shows me the nature of my ordinary self or my sick self and makes me aware of it is not my own strength, but rather the working of the great Buddha. Because I was ill, because I had no appetite, I was able to learn this crucial lesson.

In Buddhism it is said there are four ways to view water. In the same water, a heavenly being sees a precious pearl, a dragon sees a palace, a hungry spirit sees blood, and a human being sees water.

The Seventeen-Article Constitution promulgated by Prince Shotoku (574–622) contains the passage: "If he is right, you are wrong. If you are right, he is wrong. You are not quite a saint. He is not quite an idiot. Both are ordinary people."

As long as human beings continue to be human beings, we will be unable to escape from our mundane way of looking at things. If we believe our personal way of seeing things is absolutely right, and if we persist in this, allowing ourselves to be totally carried away by our own viewpoint, then a vast distance will separate us from the Pure Land, or Other Shore, and we will remain in a world of suffering on This Shore.

"Dark is the shadow of the pine made by the moonlight," writes the poet. Because of the great light of the Buddha, we are able to wake up to the darkness of our own shadows. Encompassed by that light, we are able to live with our shadows. Is this not what could be called the meditative life?

A Brocade Cannot Be Woven in One Color

It was the day of the tea ceremony during which a jar containing a year's supply of tea is opened. I decided to hang a scroll on which was written a poem by Sumita Oyama, who introduced Santoka Taneda, the famous haiku poet and priest, to the world. The poem read, "One persimmon remaining on the tree, snow on the distant mountains."

On entering this room, a guest reverently inspected the scroll and then inquired, "How do you read the second line?" The characters in that line were unaligned and one was missing. The entire work evoked an ineffable impression of artlessness. I forgot about bringing out refreshments and began to talk.

In the words of Murata Juko (1422-1502), known as the founder of the tea ceremony, "When the line wavers and characters are omitted and sufficient empty white space surrounds the work, the effect is superior. When there are no missing characters and the lines run straight, then what results is truly inferior.''

What a paradox! Ordinarily, people who practice calligraphy go to great pains to achieve perfect alignment and would consider missing characters inexcusable. At any rate, there is another viewpoint that regards unaligned and missing characters as interesting and perfection as dull. What could be the source of such thinking?

Juko also said, ''A moon without clouds is disappointing.'' Living one hundred fifty years earlier than Juko was Yoshida Kenko, author of *Tsurezure-gusa* (Essays in Idleness), in which he wrote, ''I was impressed to hear the abbot Koyu say, 'Trying to have everything in perfect order is the way of inferior persons. It is better to have some disorder. When everything is carefully regulated, it's boring.' '' He also wrote, ''Are cherry blossoms to be seen only in full bloom? Is the moon to be seen only without clouds?''

In Japan, when we talk about cherry-blossom viewing, cherry blossoms must be in full bloom; if we talk about moon-viewing, it is understood that the moon has to be full. But it is possible to enjoy buds before they open, or to enjoy the scene of the petals floating to the ground in the wind or, even more so, to savor the bare trees in winter, bereft of leaves. Rather than a bright moon in a cloudless, clear night sky, what about a moon adorned with clouds; how about the enjoyment of a crescent moon rather than a full moon, or anticipation of a moon not yet risen, or the charming thought of a moon that has just set? All things are in a state of constant flux. Our attitude toward viewing cherry blossoms or the moon reflects the enjoyment and savoring of all the vicissitudes of life just as they are.

This discussion does not refer only to the aesthetic world of the moon, cherry blossoms, calligraphy, and so on. Some children die even though their parents gave them loving care. A husband, shouldering all the responsibilities of his family, may collapse from sudden illness at the peak of his career.

Life goes on without regard to our partial or selfish desires. Accordingly, joy and anger, sadness and happiness, love and hate, and all kinds of thoughts and emotions are woven together. If everything, including misfortune, illness, and failure, is unconditionally accepted as it is, then all experience may be constructively enjoyed.

The merciful world of the Buddha embraces all people exactly as they are. It is a world in which people who swear they will never be deluded but who will soon fall into bewilderment are generously embraced as they are by the Buddha. If one wished to express this concept on a scroll, I would suggest the words ''Meandering lines and missing letters make it more interesting.''

This brings to mind a phrase from the *Shoyo-roku* (The Book of Equanimity): ''A woven brocade contains all colors.''

Birth, old age, illness, and death, as well as happiness and misfortune, gain and loss, love and hate, all these are important tools for weaving the brocade of human life. A brocade cannot be woven with the single color of happiness. Given time, place, and occasion, everything "contains all colors." It is in this way that the Pure Land, the Other Shore, is made manifest.

A Rough Experience

"Abbess, please come up," a nun cried out.

From her strained voice, I sensed that there was something wrong and hurried up to the lay trainees' room on the second floor. A bloodstained quilt cover lay crumpled on the floor and blood was spread over three of the tatami mats. Bloody footprints tracked from the window to the roof below.

The evening before, a deeply troubled woman in her thirties, accompanied by her aged mother, had come for the three-day zazen retreat (*sesshin*). Our temple specializes in the training of ordained women, but it is also open to lay women during the zazen meetings held one Sunday a month, or on another occasion for three to five days every month.

On the first day, silently praying for them, I walked behind the women facing the walls, seated in meditation. That particular person was sitting splendidly in zazen. What had happened in her household? What deep anguish had driven her to finally make her way here? Indeed, there seemed to be a storm of chaos and confusion in her head great enough to topple her over. Her zazen, subduing such a storm, was ineffably silent, exquisitely beautiful. Indisputably, it was like the venerable form of the Buddha.

I wished her to sit without giving up for three days. By the strength of zazen, willing or not, the storm would subside. When the storm calmed down and the waves in her heart grew still, she would naturally come to see and hear things as they were. Such a time would come when she would be delighted at the anguish that had guided her to this temple and the teachings of the Buddha, and she would accept her past anguish in prayerful thanks. How good of her to come flying here! "Hang on. Don't give in to the storm in your head," I had thought in prayer as I passed behind her. But she did not appear for zazen that evening. I was the first to leave the meditation hall, and as I did, I turned to an older nun who immediately followed me out. I told her to check the lay trainees' room, and this is what we found out.

It was fortunate that I had sent this nun, since she had been a nurse before ordination. A younger nun might have fainted at the sight. She reported, "The loss of this amount of blood is no immediate threat to her life. Perhaps she became afraid of dying when she saw her blood. Then she heard my footsteps coming upstairs, and probably realized she couldn't escape past me, so instead went out on the roof.''

As we had assumed, she had gone from the roof of the Main Hall to the kitchen roof. The nun and the police rescued her, and she was taken to hospital in an ambulance. I asked the nun to help me clean up the blood. We used four or five buckets of water, soaking up the blood with rags. No matter how many times we changed the water, it would immediately turn crimson again.

Reciting the Heart of Wisdom Sutra to myself, my hands stained with blood, I thought: Only when driven by such agony do people turn to religion for help. Although she had taken the trouble to come to our temple, had sat in zazen with us, and heard the teachings, she had given up and tried to kill herself. But even though her mind had been overcome by a storm, she had sat in meditation with her own body, had learned the teachings with the *Shobo-genzo* in her own hands, and had heard the Buddha's teachings with her own ears.

On that same evening, she had tried to commit suicide, even while hearing us reading *Fukan Zazengi* (Rules for Zazen) during the last zazen session for the day. But a connection with the Buddha's teachings is never lost. A seed sown in such a way cannot but grow to bear fruit.

I recalled a parable from the Lotus Sutra. To cure his many sons suffering from the effects of a poison, a good doctor compounded medicines into a remedy that smelled and tasted good. Those who were not gravely ill and had not lost their senses took the medicine gladly and were able to recover. But those who had been seriously affected by the poison were not in their right minds and, not even believing themselves to be ill, refused to take the medicine.

The father was then compelled to resort to trickery. "I have to go to a far-off country on urgent business. I have prepared some medicine for you. Keep it just in case you should ever need it," he said, and left on a trip. Soon afterward he sent a messenger home, who reported to the children that their father had died of a sudden illness.

In deep sorrow, they finally recovered their senses and took the medicine their father had left for them. Thus they were able to be cured. In this story, sickness means sickness of the heart; and the medicine represents teachings on the true way to live.

If people do not meet with sadness or suffering, they will never seek for the true way of life. When they are driven into a tight corner where they can move neither forward nor backward, then they finally begin to reflect on themselves, harbor doubts about their lives, and ask themselves the question: What is the true way to live?

The awareness of our suffering or the awakening to our illness is the first step for us to seek truth. Shakyamuni Buddha held that our recognition of suffering is the first of the Four Noble Truths. Even if driven into a very tight corner, some people still do not turn to religion for help.

Those who do so are fortunate. I wish that, guided by torment, they would break the outer shell of their little selves and discover that wider world in which they could live.

In another story, a person wishing to commit suicide entered the mountains, hung a rope from a tree limb, and put his head in the noose. As his body was about to float into space, a wooden clog slipped from one foot. Noticing his foot's unconscious efforts to feel for the clog, he became aware of the strength of that innate part of himself that was living with all its might, without regard to his self-centered thoughts of just seconds before. He then abandoned the idea of suicide.

Eiichi Enomoto wrote this poem, called "Hermit Crab":

> This shell is not of my own making.
> Borrowing it from heaven and earth,
> I live out each and every day.

One's life is a combination of what one borrows and what one is gifted with. Without borrowing all the strength of heaven and earth, one cannot truly live, even for a moment. Lack of this borrowed strength makes impossible the utterance of words, the perception through eyes and ears, the voluntary movement of arms and legs, and the involuntary working of the heart and stomach. One's awareness of this truth impels one to reject suicide.

When we are able to open our eyes to this magnificent truth, we will accept in gratitude the unhappiness and adversity which have guided us to the truth, and we will see in life's reversals the venerable form of the Buddha. Wishing and praying for her to attain that stage and awaken, I continued to wipe up the blood, which had deeply stained the tatami mats and the futon mattress.

A line from the Kannon Sutra happened to come to mind: "Kannon Bodhisattva moves at will throughout the *saha*-world." *Saha* in Sanskrit means suffering, and the *saha*-world means the world of suffering or this world, which is to be endured. The word suggests that this world is full of pain and grief and is a place we have to endure. Plunging into this world of suffering, some people are active in relieving others. Their hands become stained with blood and their bodies smeared with filth. A person making it a pleasure to be engaged in such work is called Kannon Bodhisattva.

Burning Ourselves

On cold winter mornings, I sometimes find it hard to light a candle. I must slowly melt the wax surrounding the wick. The lit candle will then burn brightly and continue to burn, melting with the heat of its own light.

And so it is with human beings. At first, we must have a good teacher to guide us and "light us," but after that, by "burning ourselves" with our own efforts, we emit light and warmth around us. However earnestly someone else urges us to burn, unless we burn ourselves, nothing will be accomplished.

One of the best Japanese Christian poets, Jukichi Yagi (1898–1927), wrote:

> There is nothing to be found,
>   even if I search.
> There is nothing to do
>   but to warm myself on my own.
> There is nothing to do
>   but to burn my own body and
>   light the place around me.

There is nothing you can do but go your own way in life, walking on your own two feet. There is nothing you can depend on, nothing to help you. There is nothing but to stand erect, resisting any temptation to depend on others.

The Blue Bird

> Though I searched all day for spring,
>   I could not find it.
> Carrying my staff,
>   I crossed over mountain after mountain.
> Coming back home,
>   I happened to grasp a spray of plum
>   blossoms.
> There I saw spring, blooming at its tip.

I believe that was written by the Chinese poet Tai-i of the Sung dynasty. A poem by the Japanese poet Bokusui Wakayama (1885–1928) reflects the same sentiment:

> Crossing mountains and rivers,
> In a country where loneliness never ends,
> I am still traveling.

In Europe, the German poet Carl Busse (1872–1918) treats a similar theme in one of his poems, as does Maurice Maeterlinck (1862–1949) in his *L'Oiseau bleu* (The Blue Bird). Whether in the East or the West, all people have sought happiness; they have searched continuously for it.

So many of these people thought of happiness as money and spent their lives chasing after wealth. Many others thought happiness lay in fame or good health, or in raising children. But for most of them life ended like an unfinished dream; only a very few became aware that true happiness is not in satisfying all our mundane desires.

Human desires escalate without limit. It is impossible to try to satisfy all of them. No matter how much you want to escape poverty, no matter how hard you work, there will be times when you can scarcely get enough food for the day. And no matter how much you hate illness, there will be times when you have to suffer from illness. Even if that illness brings you to death, there is no escape. Such is life.

If happiness is not attained unless human desires are completely fulfilled, then there is no place where you can find happiness. True happiness is never so imperfect and never depends on conditions. Even if you are deathly ill or suffering in extreme poverty, if you accept things just as they are—as happiness—with confidence that whatever happens is fine, and you make that attitude a part of yourself, I believe that you will have found real happiness.

This is what Shakyamuni Buddha searched for and discovered; it is the central truth of the teachings he expounded. He searched for happiness so earnestly that he abandoned worldly life. He was the prince of a kingdom, however small, and enjoyed all the fame and fortune he could desire. The beautiful princess Yasodhara was his wife, and he had a young son, Rahula. But in spite of this, he abandoned it all and sought the Way in the guise of a beggar.

Some time later, after attaining buddhahood, Shakyamuni told his disciple Anuruddha, "No one in the world searches for happiness more than I do."

He said on another occasion:

> Renounce trivial pleasures
> And you will encounter great happiness.
> The wise will aspire to great happiness,
> Renouncing trivial pleasures.
>
> (Dhammapada, verse 290)

Nothing Is to Be Added

On *risshun,* the first day of spring according to the lunar calendar, I arranged a branch of plum blossoms, just about to open, in a vase in the alcove. The joy from this first breath of spring filled my heart, and I felt it to be the ultimate of luxuries. Time after time I had stood under the boughs of the plum tree in the frigid air, thinking to myself how slow they were to blossom. Only a person who has waited impatiently for the slightest faint swelling in the buds will know this joy. I am able to find joy here because the gardens and fields in my temple accord with nature and its constant revolution of spring, summer, autumn, and winter.

Throughout the year, florists and grocers sell a great variety of flowers and vegetables raised in greenhouses. Children growing up in an environment out of touch with nature are totally unable to recognize the promise of flowers blooming in early spring, despite bitter cold, or grasses flowering in the gentle autumn wind.

At the store, flowers bloom out of season and all kinds of fruits and vegetables are on display throughout the year. In the modern world, the thrill of seeing flowers bloom after a long winter, or the feeling of tenderness toward the last remaining flowers of autumn, cannot be experienced. Much less do we know the joy of picking the very first tomatoes and cucumbers of the season, or of tasting them after offering them on the Buddhist altar at home. We no longer know the joy of scooping up a fish in a net while feeling the pull of the stream on our legs; we do not feel pity when the fish dies.

From the beginning we are cut off from the natural environment, which cultivates these emotions in our hearts, and it all starts with the idea that we can get anything we want with money. That cannot enrich emotions. As the words "Mother Earth" suggest, human beings are the earth's children, nature's children. What kind of adults will modern children become, deprived of such a vital sense of nature, raised in an arid environment? In what direction will the society they build go? Just to imagine it sends chills up and down my spine.

What has produced this environment? Our desires—always wanting to see the flowers we love and to eat our favorite fruits and vegetables—became entangled with another common human desire, that is, to make profits. To fulfill those desires, scientific technology has been utilized without control. In the end, everything is made available for commercial sale, resulting in an inherently lifeless world. We must not forget that people living in such a situation gradually grow more materialistic and unfeeling. Their hearts become, as it were, plasticized, and have no room for the Buddhist truth that life and death, as they are, is nirvana.

Zen Master Kosho Uchiyama said, "The original Way needs nothing to be added, nor is it clogged up. It perfectly suffices in itself. Because human beings have the ability to think, they always want to add something, and soon everything gets clogged up.'' Civilization today is clogged up as a result of the human desire to add more and more. Unless we change direction, before long there will no longer be human beings on our planet.

With the guidance of the Buddha's doctrine encompassing the laws of heaven and earth, we must revive the human heart that is moved by one flower, a heart that cries at the death of an insect. Such a heart takes great care of one's own life, other people's lives, and life in all things.

Beautiful Words

If we hear the word "stylish," we think of clothing or personal belongings or make-up, and verbal style does not immediately come to mind. But if an elegantly attired lady should happen to use bad language, even her dress loses its beauty instantly.

"Stylish words" can never be mastered overnight. The contemporary critic Tsunatake Furuya said, "I'd like to have a love for words''; and "We must be conscious of the nuances of the words we ourselves use.''

Not long ago, one of my friends left the world, never to return. Another friend announced the news to me by saying, "She is deceased.'' Later, a different friend said, "She passed away." I felt that there was a very large gulf between the two ways of saying the same thing. Here I saw reflected the difference in the personalities of these two friends. "She is deceased" seems to be an official, indifferent report with a cold ring to it. The words "she passed away," on the other hand, showed more sympathy.

Words reveal the personality of the speaker, just as facial expressions do. High-flown language often seems false and even ugly. Beautiful words are appropriate and full of warm consideration. They are alive, springing naturally from a beautiful soul.

The Buddhist priest and scholar Kazuyoshi Kino, one of the guest lecturers at my temple, Muryo-ji, once said, "Don't use language that amounts only to noise." That made a deep impression on me.

Usually, we speak only those kinds of words. That may be all right if they stay at the level of innocent noise. But in some cases, even a single inconsiderate word gives someone a wound that will fester for the rest of his or her life. Through language in our daily lives we hurt others and others hurt us. We speak and then regret what we have said; though regretting, we still speak.

Before speaking to people, Shakyamuni Buddha was always careful of the following three points. First of all, he considered whether his speech was true and, second, whether it would benefit the hearer. After making sure of its truth and benefit, he finally selected the most suitable time and place. In some cases, even if something is true, it may be better not to tell the person with whom you are speaking. It could cause him harm if the time or place is inappropriate. Shakyamuni Buddha was so careful that he applied these principles even to the utterance of a single word.

Beautiful words spring naturally from a considerate and beautiful life. Truly "stylish words" must be based on such a philosophy.

Enjoyment Along the Way

Although I know I should constantly pick the weeds that grow in the temple grounds throughout the year, I do it only by fits and starts. I'm always falling behind, and sometimes it takes me longer than expected to catch up. If I neglected this duty for a while, there would soon be so many weeds that the place would look uninhabited. Once I even resorted to a weedkiller, although I dislike weedkillers.

It must have been a strong weedkiller. For a whole year no weeds came up. Nor did moss. For several months after I began using the weedkiller, nothing would grow in that barren earth. The sight of it saddened me and made me think of human presumption.

I prayed for the weeds to come back, thinking I would not mind exhausting myself with weed picking, if only the weeds would come back. "Good

Earth," I prayed, "come quickly back to life and give life to the weeds."

The following year, weeds began to come up. So did moss. As I gazed thankfully at them I wanted to say, "I am glad you have come back all right."

Being alive is wonderful. Because they live, beautiful flowers bloom and weeds grow. It is human selfishness that considers flowers good and weeds bad. It is not their fault. Zen Master Dogen said, "A flower falls, even though we love it; and a weed grows, even though we do not love it." Humans are a nuisance to plants.

If people would just discard their selfish criteria and look carefully at flowers and grasses, they would see that heaven and earth bless the life of every flower and blade of grass, and that these things are wonderful. So it is with human beings. Because they live, people experience gain and loss, love and hatred, joy and anger, relief and sorrow. Each of these experiences is an important tool in our irreplaceable lives.

Hideo Kobayashi, a cultural critic, says that a leaf from a tree can hide the moon. If we place a leaf over our eyes, it is so close that we cannot see it as it is. A leaf over our eyes can shut out the moon and the world around us, too. If we hold the leaf away from us, however, we see the leaf as it is. So it is with other things. Mountains, rivers, the moon, clouds—all are visible if we remove the leaf from our eyes.

When it comes to things in our own lives, they can be too close to be seen in a proper perspective.

We easily get caught up in situations, carried away, eventually losing our perspective. We can be easily puffed up with pride over a trifle, or become prey to melancholy. But if we see things in perspective, we can appreciate the wonderful scenery around us.

Purifying the Heart

Once I invited to my temple seventy people from a home for the aged in Tokyo. In our mountain temple there is only one mirror. The women lined up for it in the morning to apply their make-up. People of all ages seem to want to keep their looks. But what are cosmetics? What is beauty? Physical beauty is something one is endowed with. Make-up only creates "made-up" beauty, which fades with age or loose living. Make-up washes off. I think that the kind of physical beauty that increases as one grows older and that does not wash off is the one we consider ideal.

What is the secret of beauty? Purifying the heart. A heart is not purified in a day or two, six months, or a year. It is said that a person is responsible for his looks after the age of forty. If you are turning forty tomorrow and in a hurry to do something about your looks, it is too late. Your strivings and the way you have lived over the past forty years are revealed in your face. Throughout the past forty years an invisible chisel has been shaping your face night and day; as you were happy, angry, or sad, the chisel made its marks. The kind of marks depended on what was inside you, and they will have given you the kind of beauty or ugliness that make-up can hardly conceal.

The early twentieth-century poet and feminist writer Akiko Yosano was not endowed with beauty, but it is said that she grew beautiful with age. She fell in love with a poet named Tekkan and eloped with him. They had many children and lived in great poverty. While encouraging her husband in his work, she devoted herself to literature and writing poetry. Akiko's devotion and hard life purified her mentally and physically, bringing out her spiritual luster.

By making the best of every day, we can grow old beautifully.

You Are Now at Your Youngest

"The New Year has come, and I'm older. Really, Abbess, at my age I feel depressed by what's ahead. I cannot move the way I want to, and I'm forgetful."

An old man said that to me in the lobby of a place where I had just lectured to a group of elderly people. As I warmed my hands around a hot cup of green tea, I spoke just as though talking to myself.

"I, too, am beginning to feel the ravages of time. My back and legs aren't good; I'm terribly forgetful. I really hate it. At any rate, even if I think about how I used to have a really good memory and wonder how it got this way, things never go back to what they were. I can't expect to regain my good memory. But one shouldn't talk idly. I decided to make a change. Instead of looking back, I started looking ahead. In the life that is left me, I am right now at my youngest. In an hour I'll be an hour older. Tomorrow my body and mind will be a day older. So I decided that there's nothing but to do my very best right now. I always think this way." The old man said, "That's what we've really wanted to know."

As we grow older, it is harder for us to have dreams for the future. We are apt to think only of the past. If the present is miserable and the past was happy, we try to forget the present by recalling the past. The happier the past, the more wretched the present may seem. Our happy past is no help to us now. Conversely, people who have led a sad or shameful life are so heavily burdened by their past that they can hardly stand up. But there is no need to shoulder a useless load. Whatever our past, if we are happy now, then everything is fine. Whether we benefit from our experiences depends on our attitude toward the present.

Our experiences have made us what we are, and we must live with them. All experiences are precious. We must see them as assets that enrich our lives.

Young people live eagerly for the future. The future as a guidepost for today is important, but if we dwell too much on the future and take no heed of the present, the all-important future will never come. Only if we live fully in the present can we face the future realistically.

In the words of the Chinese poet Han-shan:

> Our life span is scarcely a hundred years,
> Yet we always harbor a thousand griefs.

We often worry unnecessarily. For instance, we may worry about getting sick. When we are sick we worry that we will get worse. We worry that a minor illness could become a major one. We lose our appetites, which makes us grow worse and depresses those around us. This is no way to go through an illness. If we have to be ill, let us meet it head on. Let us welcome our illness with open arms. Let us live in such a way that we are grateful that our illness helps us improve our character. We should use the time of our illness to think about aspects of life that escaped us when we were healthy. Illness can be pleasant and rewarding when it is met as a challenge. Being sick is a joy, not suffering. The more painful it is, the more it is pleasant and enriching. By taking this attitude, we can convert our experience of illness into an asset. Is this not what could be called ''living zazen''?

At the end of a meal with some visitors, I looked at the remaining tea in my cup and said, ''For example, even in talking about a cup of tea, there is a vast difference between saying 'only this much is left' and 'this much is still left.' The first attitude is negative and gloomy, the second positive and cheerful. Just by changing our attitude a little, wouldn't we see life quite differently?''

I read a book by the poet Setsuko Kurobe, about a mother whose child had congenital brain damage. The child liked pictures. Perhaps all the child could do was draw pictures. But instead of talking about how little the child could do, the mother talked happily to Setsuko about how much the child could do.

Setsuko herself cannot use her right hand. A therapist told her, ''You have a left hand, don't you? Try to practice writing. You can write far better than most people.'' Setsuko wrote, ''I think not of what I cannot do, but of what I am able to do.'' I cannot forget these words.

If we just try to change our attitude a little and look at the other side of things, what we gain replaces what we lost. A situation can be changed from an embarrassment to a cause for celebration.

Hearing the Wind in the Pines

When the ceremony marking the completion of the major restoration of Todai-ji, the famous temple in Nara, was shown on a television news program, there was a shot of a bronze votive lantern (designated a National Treasure) on which is etched the figure of a boy playing a flute. The lantern stands at the side of the road leading to the temple. The figure of the boy playing a flute immediately reminded me of Zen Master Sodo

Yokoyama, who was fond of grass whistles. On another television program, "The Grass Whistle Sermon" in the Religious Hour series, Zen Master Yokoyama and I engaged in a dialogue. Soon after the program I received a letter from a viewer, who wrote, "The dialogue between you and Zen Master Yokoyama was as inspiring as a great work of art."

I shall always remember Yokoyama's words when I visited him at his home. "When I said to a child, 'I can make a whistle out of any blade of grass,' the child asked, 'Can you make a whistle out of a pine needle?' But it is the wind that makes the pines sing, you know. The voice of the wind in the pines is the most beautiful sound there is. The wind should make pine needles sing instead of me. Either the wind or I can do it. When the wind roars, it is the universe that makes it roar. Whether a voice is loud or soft, it is the voice of the universe. Even silence has a voice, and a mountain has its own particular 'mountain' voice."

Now Zen Master Yokoyama is dead, and the trees and grasses at his home and the wind in the universe are probably blowing whistles in his place. But I wonder if a visitor would hear in those whistles the voice of the universe, the voice of the Buddha, and the sound of Zen Master Yokoyama's grass whistle.

The wind goes its own way and is without form. We know it is there when we hear it in the grass or trees, see the clouds scudding overhead, or feel it blow against us.

We cannot see or hear autumn, or hold it in our hands. But when the leaves turn red and the ears of rice turn golden, they signal the arrival of autumn. When we hear the crickets chirping at night or an autumn shower striking the eaves, or pick ripe apples and persimmons, we embrace autumn. Autumn becomes something to savor.

The life and voice of the Buddha is everywhere in heaven and earth, and is manifested in all things. As art historian Muneyoshi Yanagi (1889–1961) wrote in his last years in his book *Shin-ge* (Verses of the Heart), "Buddha is the name of something nameless." The life of the Buddha originally had neither name nor form, and is in everything, from a tree or a blade of grass to a tile or a stone. It becomes the wind in the pines or in a sail; it is born as man or woman; it is in good and evil, beauty and ugliness. Whatever form something takes, it manifests the Buddha. The magically gifted monkey in sixteenth-century China's greatest comic novel could not leave the palm of the Buddha's hand, nor can we.

Whenever I am so arrogant as to think that I have the power to give myself life, I think of this poem by a five-year-old child:

> The moment I say, "Tongue, speak!"
> My tongue has moved.
> When I told my tongue to speak,
> What moved it?

The power that moves my tongue before I do is a power that works without rest when I sleep and makes a flower bloom or a horse neigh. Whether we know it or not, the Buddha holds us in the palm of his hand, and he is the power that gives us life. To symbolize and revere that power, people have given artistic form to what originally was without name or form, by carving images of buddhas and bodhisattvas in human form. In the way a child sometimes needs to call its mother, we call on Amida Buddha or Kannon Bodhisattva. Then everything is revealed as Amida or as transformations of Kannon.

One hot summer day on Mount Ma-ku in China, Zen Master Pao-ch'e sat fanning himself. A young Zen monk approached him and said, "The nature of wind is everywhere. There is no place it is not. Why do you use a fan?" The master answered, "Although you know that the nature of wind is everywhere, you do not yet know the nature of there being no place it is not." The young monk asked, "Then what is the nature of there being no place it is not?" The Zen master just sat fanning himself in silence. Silently fanning oneself is a valuable practice.

However well we understand that we manifest the life of the Buddha, we cannot realize our full potential unless we practice the Buddha's teachings. Still, the life of the Buddha is manifested in us regardless of whether we understand or are aware of it or practice the Buddha's teachings. It is manifested in us as we go about our daily lives; for instance, when we conserve water or plant life, or tackle our household chores wholeheartedly.

Whether a dewdrop is on a flower or a heap of dung, the morning light sparkles on it just the same. What a joy it is to know that our finite lives are part of the infinite lives of the Buddha!

About two hundred years ago, the folklore scholar Sugae Masumi (1754–1829) visited Muryo-ji, the temple where I live, and dedicated this poem to our principal image of Amida Buddha:

> When I asked about the immeasurable age of
>   the Buddha
> In the presence of the Buddha,
> Answer came from the wind in the pines.

Every time I read this poem, my heart is renewed, and I strain to hear the wind in the pines, feeling I must live every moment in a way that creates wind in the pines.

An Eye-opening

Since mountains were the theme of the New Year's poetry party at the Imperial Palace, in the alcove of our temple I hung a calligraphy scroll that reads "Sitting alone like a great mountain," as an early-spring decoration. During China's T'ang dynasty (618–907), a Buddhist monk visited Zen Master Pai-chang, who was living on Mount Ta-hsiung-feng, and asked him, "What is the most splendid thing in the world?" The Zen master answered, "Sitting alone like a great mountain, as I am doing right now."

What am I doing right now? This is the most important question we can ask ourselves to determine our direction in life. We are not all saints, and how many of us can always be confident that right now we are doing the right thing? At times we might do inane things or lose our temper. If so, what a miserable way to live, and what a waste of irretrievable time. Yet some people are unaware of how they live, while growing older with each passing year.

That point is illustrated in a poem by a schoolboy named Sunaga:

> In the middle of Japan, surrounded by
> The Pacific Ocean, the Sea of Okhotsk,
> The Japan Sea, and the East China Sea,
> At Furukawa First Elementary School,
> Right now I am fighting.

Hardly more than specks of dust on this earth, we get angry and quarrel over trifles. We are carried away by our emotions. If we could see ourselves with complete detachment, we would feel as if we were sitting alone like a great mountain, because we would be seeing ourselves with the Buddha's eyes.

Neglect Is the Road to Death

About thirty years ago, a worshipper donated to our temple a large hanging scroll depicting Fudo

Myoo, protector of Buddhism, painted by Ryusen Miyahara. He was one of the best Japanese artists of his time, and one of the most prolific painters of Buddhist themes. I forgot for a long time that our temple had it. When I remembered, I brought it out and had it mounted. I asked Miyahara, then seventy-seven, to write the title of the painting and sign his name on the box for the scroll. He confessed, "I painted this nearly forty years ago and I'm ashamed of it now. It's not something that should be hung up for others to see. If it were in my possession, I'd burn it." I received a letter from him soon afterward, in which he wrote, "The way of art is endless. All I can do now is try as best I can."

I was deeply touched by the words of Miyahara, who was so devoted to his art and so hard on himself. He had dedicated his life to art, devoting every hour of every day to his endeavor. The evolution of his style over the past forty years has been remarkable.

Shakyamuni Buddha says:

> Endeavor is the eternal way.
> Neglect is the way to death.
> People who spur themselves on happily
>   never die.
> People wallowing in self-indulgence,
> Even though they have life,
> Are as if dead already.
>
> (Dhammapada, verse 21)

We should make every moment of life worthwhile. Just eating and sleeping, living without purpose, and dying in that state make us "human-manure-producing machines," according to Zen Master Kodo Sawaki. Even dogs and cats can lead such a life. But it is just too miserable, and it is inexcusable to waste a precious life that way. We can find out if someone is alive by seeing whether he is breathing, but here I refer to a higher level of living.

Those who try wholeheartedly to do what human beings should do through allotted tasks go on living eternally, even after the body dies. (There are various kinds of "allotted tasks." Seeking wealth, fame, or love is not an allotted task in the Buddhist sense.) As for people who are physically strong and rejoice in their youth, but are self-indulgent and waste time, their body is worth no more than bleached bones lying in a field. Some people live each day as if it had the value of a hundred years. Others may live a hundred years miserably, with as little to show for it as if they had lived only a single day. Some, by discarding what is unnecessary, ennoble themselves; while others, living in degradation, abase themselves. Among so many possibilities, we should try to live at least one day in a manner that gladdens the hearts of the buddhas.

Illness is good; failure is good; let wind and waves be as they are. Growing spiritually and becoming more radiant with each passing day, I would like to live every hour as if it were a day.

Looking for the Self

One spring afternoon a group of thirty young couples were enjoying themselves in a beautiful forest. All the couples but one were married; an unmarried young man came with a harlot. The young people were of good family and properly educated. As they lost themselves in their amusements, the harlot slipped away with their belongings. The young people ran all through the woods in search of her and came upon a holy man quietly seated in meditation under a tree. They approached him and asked, "Venerable one, have you seen a woman?" He inquired, "Young ones, why are you looking for her?" They explained everything to him.

The holy man inquired further, "My young people, which do you think is more important, to seek that woman or to seek your true selves?"

The unexpected question left the young people at a loss for words. Earlier, they had been entirely wrapped up in their own pleasures, forgetting themselves. When questioned by the holy man, they came to themselves and replied instinctively, "Needless to say, to seek our true selves."

"Sit down here, and I will expound to you the true teachings," said the holy man, and he began to teach them the meaning of the true self and what we should do with the true self. Like a blessed rain falling on parched earth, his teachings entered deeply into their pure hearts. They rejoiced to become his disciples.

The holy man was none other than Shakyamuni Buddha.

Zen Master Dogen said, "To study the Way is to study the self." The Buddha taught his disciples to rely on the Law and oneself, but not on others."

> Self is the refuge of self.
> What else could be our refuge?
> A well-regulated self becomes a refuge
> Such as few can find.
>
> (Dhammapada, verse 160)

Some people think that money is the key that opens all doors, or something like that. They think that money provides security or that fame can make life worth living. Or if not money or fame, then a loving husband or wife, children, or doting parents. Just what is the self, which we can rely on better than money, fame, or family? It would seem to be a petty self that easily cries and complains. A well-regulated self does not.

Looking for a Good Teacher

Zen Master Dogen wrote in his *Gakudo Yojin-shu* (Instructions on Learning the Way): "A disciple can be compared to a good piece of wood, and a master to a carpenter. Even good wood will not show its fine grain unless worked on by a good carpenter. Even a warped piece of wood, in the hands of a good carpenter, shows the results of good craftsmanship."

Dogen showed the importance of finding a good or a true teacher by comparing the master-disciple relationship to a carpenter and his wood. He even went so far as to say that if we could not find a good teacher, it would be better not to study at all. This is severe, but true.

Liking or disliking a subject in school often depends on the teacher. I am struck by the importance of a good teacher and the difficulty of finding one, whether it is a teacher of the tea ceremony or flower arrangement, one who teaches on the job, or a teacher of life itself.

Good teachers know deep in their hearts the boundlessness of the Way. They also know their own pettiness and lack of compassion as compared to the height and breadth of the Way. Accordingly, good teachers do not put on airs. True teachers cannot be recognized by appearance. Only true teachers tell us things we do not like to hear. Without assuming any authority, they dress plainly and live in a simple dwelling, making the Way their teacher, the Dharma their teacher. Single-mindedly, they continue to seek and practice the Way.

The last words of such a great teacher as Shakyamuni Buddha were: "I am not your teacher. Your teacher is the Dharma, the true teachings."

We are supported in our search by the warm words of Zen Master Dogen: "Regardless of how difficult or painful the training may be, students [of Zen who are weak-willed in seeking the Way] should seek their (good practitioners') guidance."

Encouraged by another of his sayings, "What we earnestly wish can be accomplished," we have to rub the sleep from our eyes and go on looking for the good teacher, the right teacher.

Self-restraint

In the presence of others we try to behave sensibly and modestly. But when we are alone we may do ridiculous things, which show what we are really like. Although we think we are alone, the Buddha is watching, the gods are watching, Heaven is watching, and another self within us is watching.

If we do something good when no one is looking, we wish to be praised or recognized, and we go around telling people what we have done. If we are not appreciated or are slandered, we are disappointed and feel that what we have done is less worthwhile. When we have done something bad, we are afraid that others may find out, and so we try our best to hide it. If we have managed to hide it, we feel we have gained something.

However, it is quite easy to deceive people. And their opinions are often quite baseless. As long as we let the viewpoint of others serve as the measure of our acts, our lives will be wasted. Moreover, though we may do something only in accordance with other people's opinions, the fact of our action remains a fact, which will eternally make up one page in our life, serving as either a positive or negative factor in the formation of our character.

Whether good or bad, whatever we do remains a fact, which does not increase or diminish in value according to the praise or blame of others; it becomes a karmic force that accompanies us. In this way, our personality is unfailingly shaped by all our acts.

Undisturbed by praise or censure and taking that universal truth deeply to heart, we fervently wish to act always with prudence. This ardent desire is accomplished through self-restraint.

Because I know that this is extremely difficult to do, I will keep these words firmly in mind and try to be very careful with each day.

From Possession to Possessor

Money, fame, a husband or wife, children, all these are considered sources of happiness. Those are all one's possessions. In a lifetime, they are the possessions that may change with age and the different costumes we wear as we get older. Then we notice that we have forgotten the all-important owner, the possessor of those possessions.

Possessions being impermanent, it is a matter of course that they change or disappear. Life changes to death; love may turn to hatred; youth turns to old age; an obedient child may turn on his parents; a mountain of savings may turn to a heap of loans. That is the natural state of the world of impermanence. Seeking true happiness in such bubble-like, impermanent possessions is mistaken from the very beginning. The philosopher and political theorist Jean-Jacques Rousseau wrote in *Émile: Où de l'éducation:* "One is not born a king, a noble, a courtier, or a man of possession. Everyone is born naked and poor. . . . He is destined to die."

For a period of time, from birth to the end of life, we assume various kinds of costumes, such as the splendid attire of a queen, a beggar's tatters, a monk's robes, or the fine clothes of a rich man. Almost everyone goes through life dazzled by those costumes. People have completely forgotten what to do with themselves. By taking off and throwing away all those costumes, we become naked.

Shakyamuni Buddha noticed this quickly and gave up everything to renounce secular life in earnest pursuit of the right way to live as the possessor of things. In order to seek true happiness that never changes, he left the world and entered into religious practice.

The all-important factor is the attitude toward life of those who possess things. All that we need to do is to change our attitude toward life. How should we change? To put it simply, do not look beyond yourself. Do not seek happiness somewhere else or at any other time—tomorrow, next year, or in the next life. It is at all times "here and now" that we must straighten our posture and sit upright.

In the poem "Looking for Spring," which appears on p. 40, the Chinese poet Tai-i says that all day long he went about looking for spring, but he was unable to find it. He walked and walked through the mountains, but still could not find spring. Giving up, he returned home and by chance took hold of a branch of plum blossoms by the eaves of his house, where he at last found the fragrance of spring. Spring was right there at his home. That is to say, it was not necessary to go out searching for it. As long as we look beyond ourselves, we will never find permanent happiness.

Even if you are ordained and renounce secular life, nothing will come of it as long as you look beyond yourself. Everything will be the same. The only thing to do is to sit back, wherever you are, and always accept what is given.

True Happiness

Worldly people are always running around in search of happiness. The kinds of happiness are defined; stages of happiness are pursued, studied scientifically, philosophized about. Things even go so far as politicians debating on the best forms of government. The same is true with religion. In Buddhism, true happiness is referred to as "crossing over to the Other Shore," "paradise," "peace of mind," or "Rebirth in the Pure Land." These expressions differ, but they mean that people seek happiness. The fundamental differences are in the kinds of happiness people seek.

During a sermon by Shakyamuni Buddha, his

cousin and disciple, Anuruddha, fell asleep. As soon as the sermon was over, Shakyamuni called Anuruddha to his side and reprimanded him. Anuruddha felt deep repentance and vowed never to sleep again. In his struggle to stay awake, he eventually went blind. In spite of this, as the Buddha's disciple he still had to sew his own surplice.

"Would someone looking for happiness please thread this needle for me?" Anuruddha murmured, blinking his sightless eyes and poking at the eye of the needle.

"Let me thread it for you," someone offered, approaching Anuruddha. The speaker was none other than Shakyamuni Buddha.

Anuruddha started with surprise: "I am unworthy of your kindness. I wouldn't dream of bothering you with threading this needle. But . . . could *you* really be looking for happiness?" Anuruddha found himself blurting out.

The Buddha answered quietly, "No one in the world searches for happiness more than I do."

The happiness worldly people seek is in wealth rather than poverty, health rather than sickness, success rather than failure, gain rather than loss, beauty rather than ugliness, and love rather than hatred. Most people, in the midst of endless vicissitudes, look for satisfaction beyond themselves. However, no matter what they fervently desire, in real life good fortune and bad fortune are all interwoven. In real life, all things take their course, regardless of our personal circumstances.

Shakyamuni Buddha saw this truth with enlightened eyes. His first step in pursuit of the Way was his abandonment of everything that ordinary people regarded as sources of happiness. Renouncing his princely title, giving up his wife and child, he set out on his quest as a mere mendicant monk. After six years of religious practice, he singled out the results and taught that as long as one looks beyond oneself for happiness, it cannot be found. Whatever our situation—poverty, illness, or other kinds of hardship—we must accept it as a blessing, just as it is.

I once heard a story about a visit to heaven and hell. In both places the visitor saw many people seated at a table on which many delicious foods were laid out. Chopsticks over a meter long were tied to their right hands, while their left hands were tied to their chairs. In hell, however much they stretched out their arms, the chopsticks were too long for them to get food into their mouths. They grew impatient and got their hands and chopsticks tangled with one another's. The delicacies were scattered here and there.

In heaven, on the other hand, people happily used the long chopsticks to pick out someone else's favorite food and feed it to him, and in turn they were being fed by others. They all enjoyed their meal in harmony.

On This Shore and the Other Shore, in heaven and hell, the problem is exactly the same. What is important is how it is solved. It all depends on the attitude with which people receive.

As long as we look beyond ourselves for the

Other Shore, paradise, happiness, the Buddha, or enlightenment, we will never find it. Only by looking within the self can we become aware of the blessings we are endowed with.

Rebirth in the Pure Land does not happen in time or space; heaven or hell depends on one's state of mind. As explained in *Fukan Zazengi* (Rules for Zazen), "Even the slightest gap between you and the Way is as great as that between heaven and earth."

> In a hamlet or in a forest,
> In deep water or on dry land,
> Wherever the enlightened dwell,
> That place is a peaceful realm.
>
> (Dhammapada, verse 98)

Discarding selfish thoughts, such as acceptance or rejection, hatred or love, I would like to face whatever happens at any time in the place I have been granted, positively accepting the here and now as my training ground and my final haven of serenity.

Endeavor

> If you do, you can.
> If you don't, you can't.
> When you say you can't do what can be done,
> It means you haven't set out to do it.

The old nun who raised me from the age of five

had a habit of murmuring this poem, not so much to encourage other people as to strengthen her own resolve. She would repeat it over and over in a low voice. The poem and the way she looked as she murmured it entered deeply into my young heart and took firm root. Without my being aware of it, the spirit of the poem seems to have fostered a great deal in me.

> Everything can be accomplished if I try.
> I have lived my life thus far by these words.

> The birds are my true teachers,
> Leading me to write by using my mouth.

These two poems were written by the Buddhist nun Junkyo Oishi. Her life demonstrates how endeavor can overcome even extreme difficulties.

In June 1904 in the red-light district of Horie in Osaka, the proprietor of a geisha house, Manjiro Nakagawa, went berserk on hearing of his wife's infidelity and put his six geisha to the sword. Five died instantly, but one, Tsumakichi, was saved by some miracle. It happened on a summer night, when Tsumakichi was seventeen. Having lost both hands and no longer able to dance as before, she joined a company of wandering entertainers.

During a tour of the north, the company moved to the city of Sendai. Tsumakichi lodged at a boardinghouse there. In the garden were a pair of canaries and their young, kept in a tiny cage in a maple tree. They had little room to fly. While the male bird sang happily at the top of his voice, the female nestled her young and fed them with her bill.

Tsumakichi thought to herself, "They do everything with their mouths, don't they! I have a mouth too. If I try my best, there shouldn't be anything I can't do with mine." She recalled the words of her foster father in Horie, the man who had cut off her arms. He had often said, "Anything other people can do, I'm sure we can. Everything depends solely on effort." She determined to start anew. Tsumakichi, who did not even know how to write, took a brush between her lips and began her desperate self-training.

Later she became a nun and took the name Junkyo Oishi. Her pictures and writings, all of which she executed by holding a brush in her mouth, were displayed in places as far off as Munich. "If the problem is a crippled body, nothing can be done about it, but don't let your heart become a cripple," is what she said to encourage other disabled people. This nun provides an excellent example of desperate endeavor supported by deep faith.

In *Shin-ge,* Muneyoshi Yanagi says, "Give it your all! Then you will have no regrets." There is nothing you cannot accomplish with the courage that is born of desperation.

In *Shobo-genzo Zuimonki,* Zen Master Dogen says that we should live each day, each hour, in the same frame of mind as that of a man falling from a horse. In that brief moment before he hits the ground, all his ability and learning is useless, and there is no time to think, no time for daydreams or self-reproach. When we face a matter of life and death, there is no time to look around or fantasize. All depends on our readiness. Zen Master Dogen said that we should live our whole lives in a state of readiness.

Worrying about how clever we are, looking around to see if there is someone somewhere who could do something for us, and stating our terms—all this is proof of not being serious. If we spoil ourselves, depend on others, and are generally passive, even a path that had been open to us will in the end be closed. If we face problems squarely, our resolution and endeavor can cause even a tightly locked door to open wide. If we do not, a door that had been wide open could slam shut. The problem lies not with others, but with ourselves.

Drop by drop, water can wear right through a rock. We can see where rain or the ceaseless flow of a river wore away a rock or even created a hole in it.

Shakyamuni Buddha said in *Yuikyo-gyo* (The Sutra of the Buddha's Last Teaching):

"Monks, if you earnestly persevere, nothing is difficult. But, above all, you must strive with all your might, like ceaselessly flowing water wearing away a rock. If your practice becomes lax, it becomes as difficult as trying to start a fire by rubbing two sticks together but stopping before the wood gets hot. Earnest perseverance is true endeavor.''

Zen Master Dogen says in the section ''The Great Practitioners' Eight Teachings for Attainment of Enlightenment'' of *Shobo-genzo* (The Treasury of the True Dharma Eye) that the fourth aspect, endeavor, signifies doing good single-mindedly and continually.

The discovery of fire and the knowledge of how to use it gave great impetus to cultural development. In ancient times the job of keeping the fire going was a serious undertaking. One of the most important tasks of the woman in each household was to keep the fire burning continuously. To get a fire started, flints had to be struck to make sparks, or two sticks were rubbed together. There can be no pause in the latter method. Similarly, if our heart stopped to rest, we would die; the sun never takes a break. And religious practice should never pause.

In Shakyamuni Buddha's time, there was a youth of good family named Sona Kolivisa. He converted to Buddhism and became a disciple of the Buddha, throwing himself into intense religious practice. He could not attain enlightenment, however. He lost confidence and became confused, wondering whether to return to the mundane world. Sona spoke of his feelings to Shakyamuni Buddha.

The Buddha quietly inquired: ''Sona, I heard that while you were still at home, you were very good at playing the harp. If the strings of the harp are stretched too tightly, isn't it true that the sound is not good?"

"Yes, sir. Not only will the tone be poor, but the strings might break."

"Well then, and if the strings are not tight enough, you cannot produce good sound either."

"That's right. When the strings are neither too tight nor too loose, the tone will be just right."

"Well, Sona, training in the Buddhist Way is the same. If you overstrain yourself, you will not have peace of mind. If you are too lax, you tend to get lazy. Sona, in this case, too, you must take the Middle Path."

The Buddha earnestly explained that endeavor means being neither impatient nor negligent.

Single-mindedness

Zen Master Dogen said that endeavor means doing good single-mindedly and continually. Simply devoting yourself to something is not true endeavor. However hard we try to satisfy our mundane desires, it is not spiritual endeavor, or endeavor in the religious sense. Even if we work without rest to gain wealth or fame, it is not endeavor in the religious sense. To do good means to be in tune with the Buddhist Way, or the natural course of the universe, and is quite different from seeking to satisfy our own desires.

Yoshio Toi, a Buddhist monk and former elementary-school principal, wrote this poem:

You might say you are living,
But even a worm is living.
Since we are human beings,
We'd like to live with a little more
    human dignity.
You might say you're living
    with all your might,
But even a caterpillar or a millipede
    lives with all its might,
And human beings should not live
    like caterpillars or millipedes.
By making just a few more people happy,
Wouldn't we be living with all our might?

The opposite of endeavor is self-indulgence. No matter how much effort it requires to fulfill the desires of the mundane self, it is still self-indulgence. If we focus our desires on the Way and selflessly follow in its path, continuing without interruption, we are engaged in endeavor in the religious sense.

Single-mindedness in relation to endeavor reminds me of a story in a lecture given by Zen Master Kodo Sawaki, which I heard shortly after I became a nun.

There was a forest fire in the mountains. Birds and beasts fled as fast as they could. Among them there was a little bird that thought she would try to put the fire out. She dipped her wings in the river, then flew over the fire again and again, sprinkling drops of water. The other birds laughed at her and said it would only exhaust her and come to nothing, but she continued anyway. That was all one small bird could do. A heavenly deity felt sympathy for the little bird and sent a great rain that put out the fire.

When doing something, we may ask ourselves if we will succeed. We may wonder about the results and what other people's reactions will be. Then we may become too afraid of making mistakes to do anything.

"To live is to grow, persisting in true endeavor, walking on, always looking forward," said the writer Yaeko Nogami when she was over eighty. She continued in old age to study German and philosophy under Hajime Tanabe, a philosopher and former professor at the University of Tokyo. I often think of her.

Cats and dogs live from day to day, eating and sleeping. We prefer a more worthwhile human existence. How do we go about it?

> Endeavor is the eternal way.
> Neglect is the way to death.
> People who spur themselves on happily
>   never die.
> People wallowing in self-indulgence,
> Even though they have life,
> Are as if dead already.
>
> (Dhammapada, verse 21)

We should constantly face forward and walk on, step by step, following the Way, without letting up. That is how to live. In these verses, the Buddha says that if we do this, we will have everlasting life, and death can never destroy us. Bustling about like slaves to greed is not a meaningful way for human beings to live and is in fact the way to death.

Walk Straight by Winding Along

A relative of mine is a potter. Every year he holds a one-man exhibition at a Tokyo department store. One year I went to see his work, and the first thing that caught my eye was a dish with thistles painted on it. Their color, a gentle yet penetrating indigo, reminded me of a shade often seen in traditionally dyed cloth. There were two thistles, one tall and one short, against a background of a cloud floating in the sky. One could almost hear the wind blowing over the peaceful highland where the thistles grew. The thistles made me think of the potter's long years of true endeavor.

He was twenty-four when first chosen a winner in the Nitten, one of Japan's most prestigious annual art exhibitions. His entry was a large ornamental jar, which he made using the same process as he had for the dish just mentioned. Like the dish, it had thistles painted on it in a dark shade of indigo. The flowers as well as the leaves and stems were large, and the thistles looked defiant, almost challenging the wind. They seemed to say, "Just try coming close and we'll stick you." That was several decades ago.

At the one-man show, the thistles painted on the dish seemed to sway before my eyes, as if bending in the wind, ready to open to the rain if it rained and completely at ease with their place in the world. They were not proud, nor did they shrink back. They had a kind of balanced elegance. While continuing with various experiments, the potter had pursued a single goal in life. As I thought of his perseverance, I felt great respect for him.

Sensing the dignity of his ceaseless endeavor reflected in those gentle thistles, I continued to stand there. Suddenly these words came back to me: "Even a chestnut tree does not grow old for nothing." I had heard them only half an hour earlier from the Buddhist priest and scholar Kazuyoshi Kino as I was about to leave his house for the exhibition. While we were enjoying some chestnut sweets together, I had told him the story of where they had come from.

The chief priest of the head temple used to be a schoolteacher. The father of a former pupil of his owns a confectionery in Nakatsugawa that makes sweets with chestnuts from a hundred-year-old tree. His former pupil thought that these chestnuts tasted quite different from those of a young tree and wanted him to try some, so one autumn he sent him a box of the sweets and has continued to do so every year.

I had not been sufficiently impressed by the thought of an old tree's chestnuts, but Kino was.

He said with deep emotion, "Even a chestnut tree does not grow old for nothing." The remark took me by surprise. I thought quickly about what I had said, and then appreciated his comment.

Taking leave of Kino, I went to the exhibition. There I saw the dish with thistles painted on it. It hinted at the passage of so many years and so many trials in the potter's life, and reminded me of the conversation about the chestnut tree. I became lost in thought. Well over ten years have passed since then, and to this day my relative the potter continues to paint thistles.

In Kyoto, Ken'ichi Sakuma has continued to copy his picture of a praying child. He has painted more than fifty-thousand copies of it. Sakuma's vigor and innocence and the potter's continued efforts remind me of Zen Master Dogen's injunction to do good single-mindedly and continually.

"Continually" does not mean without stopping. As in driving a car, when we go down the road of life we cannot expect the traffic lights always to be green. Sometimes we have to stop at the red light of illness. Even if at first we are resolute, as soon as we run into trouble and the situation looks bleak, some of us say, "It's no use," and perhaps despair and give up. But stopping, retreating, or making a wide detour is more enriching and gives us far more inner strength than traveling down a straight and easy road.

Zen Master Genshu Watanabe in his last years called to his bedside a monk who had recently become a disciple. The master asked, "How can one go straight on a steep mountain road of ninety-nine curves?" When the young disciple replied, "I don't know," he was told, "Walk straight by winding along."

When told to walk straight, we stupidly think we have to cross mountains, hills, rivers, and the sea in a straight line. Ignoring traffic lights, we dash off like a race car, looking neither left nor right. But we only deceive ourselves into thinking we progress as we lurch forward. Instead, "Go straight by winding along."

Myself, Here and Now

The opposite of endeavor is self-indulgence; as explained before, self-indulgence is based on delusion. You must eliminate all thoughts of what you would like to do and devote all your energy right here and now to the role assigned to you.

Recently I was touched by the poem "Cleaning Rag" by the poet and scholar of children's literature Michio Mado (b. 1909):

When I came back home on a rainy day,
A cleaning rag was waiting for me
   in the entrance hall.
"I'm a cleaning rag," it said,
   with a friendly look,
Though it hadn't wanted to become one.

Until quite recently it had been a shirt.
It was as soft as my skin.
Maybe in America or somewhere
It had been a cotton flower,
Smiling in the sun and the wind.

The misery in my face shows that I would much rather be a shirt than a cleaning rag. A rag that is still in the shape of a shirt is very hard to clean with. When it is a shirt, it should be a shirt for all it is worth; when it is a cleaning rag, it should work as hard as it can as a cleaning rag. This is what it means to perform one's role in life. This is true endeavor, a life spent following the Way.

Plum Blossoms Harmonize with Snow

Plum blossoms are all the more beautiful when the branches are covered with snow. They perfume the winter air. As I gazed out at some, I recalled the saying of an ancient sage: "A branch of plum blossoms harmonizes fragrantly with snow." The thought made me straighten up from being hunched over the table where I was sitting, since I realized that plum blossoms had something to teach me about life. Instead of succumbing to severe winter weather, they exude their fragrance, look noble in their garland of snow, and flourish.

A sad experience can easily discourage some people, leaving them feeling that everything has gone wrong, even taking away their courage to go on living. When they have to deal with an unpleasant situation or with suffering, some people try to escape, lie their way out of it, or blame someone else. Constantly comparing themselves with others, they may come to feel inferior. In this way, the unhappier they are, the more it warps and embitters them; eventually they may give up hope.

But consider this: plum blossoms that bloom in a greenhouse have no resistance to cold and no fragrance. Vegetables grown outside, exposed to the wind and rain, are much more delicious than those grown out of season in greenhouses.

The same may be said of human beings. What helps to enrich us and make us strong is not favorable circumstances, but failure, misfortune, or illness. What matters most is how we take misfortune. The saying "A branch of plum blossoms harmonizes fragrantly with snow" teaches us how to deal with difficult circumstances.

Zen Master Hakuin (1686–1769) wrote on a scroll, "Welcome the great Bodhisattva of Hell." If one falls ill, one should welcome the illness with thanks. If misfortune strikes, learn from it. This is how I would like to live.

A Monk's Mouth Is like a Stove's

In Dogen's *Tenzo Kyokun* (Instructions to the

Kitchen Supervisor) we find this saying of Kaccayana, a disciple of Shakyamuni Buddha: "A monk's mouth is like a stove's." More than thirty years ago, when I was a newly ordained nun and enrolled in the training temple, I would always sit behind the senior nuns. One day in a *shosan* talk after the morning sutra service, I heard that saying for the first time. At the age of fifteen I only understood it to mean that monastics should eat anything put in front of them, whether they like it or not. I thought the saying referred only to eating, and forgot about it for a long time.

Recently that saying came back to me, and without thinking I repeated it aloud. I realized that "a monk's mouth" does not have to be taken literally, but can mean the "mouth" of one's life or the "mouth" of heaven and earth and the whole universe. For instance, all kinds of experiences go into the "mouth" of one's life, including the things we dread, such as the deaths of loved ones or one's own death. How are these unwelcome things to be "burned"?

A stove takes in anything; it has no likes or dislikes. It burns alike the smoothest wood and the thorniest branches in order to steam rice, cook vegetables, or heat bath water.

All experiences enrich and purify us spiritually and physically. Joy, sorrow, failure, success, love, and hate all go into the stove of life. We should accept all our experiences and use them to benefit ourselves and other people. A stove that rejects hateful things will not burn well, and no meals can be cooked on it. Eventually it will stop functioning altogether. Its smoke will add to the problem and create a big nuisance.

While continuing to ponder over these things, one day I came across the following poem in a newspaper. It is by Eiichi Enomoto, a lay *nembutsu* practitioner who believes in salvation through Amida Buddha.

> My wastebasket accepts anything—
> Scraps of paper or my mistakes
>   in composition.
> Without a word, it just swallows them up.

A wastebasket not only accepts everything silently, but gives its contents another life, putting the waste out into the world again. A wastebasket is like the mouth of heaven and earth, or of the universe. It is like a stove in this respect. Fortune and misfortune, profit and loss—all are absorbed as one.

The life of a monk or a nun devoted to the Way of the Buddha is itself the life of the Buddha. Everyone and everything and every phenomenon in this world are in the palm of the Buddha's hand, whether they are conscious of it or not. As soon as we begin to realize this, we will be able to use failure and misfortune to enrich ourselves and live our lives fully. I have gained a new understanding of the meaning of "A monk's mouth is like a stove's."

A Cheerful Attitude

The president of a certain company told me, "For some time we had trouble with graffiti in our company restroom. No matter how many warnings we gave, no matter how many times we repainted, new graffiti appeared. Then one day we found a note on the wall there. It read, 'Please don't dirty my good workplace with your graffiti!' It was in the faltering script of our old cleaning woman. I'm sure I was not the only one moved by her protest. From that day on, there was no more writing on the walls. What neither my reprimands, as president, nor those of the executive director could prevent was stopped by that one note in an unsteady hand. We were really impressed."

"My good workplace" is a wonderful phrase. Cleaning toilets is apt to be looked down on, even by those who do it, but the cleaning woman proudly declared it important work in a good workplace. Her note indicated pride, joy, and enthusiasm for what she did. Everyone must have been taken aback by her attitude, including those who had continued to write on the walls after many warnings. She had what is termed in *Tenzo Kyokun* "Joyful Mind."

All work is good. Whether it is worthwhile depends not on what kind it is, but on the attitude of the person doing it. One should think of one's work with the same attitude as the cleaning woman did. Whatever she did, she went about it cheerfully. If we approach work with the same attitude, it will be a success.

Parental Mind

As part of my practice of gratitude, I once had the duty of being a cook for the length of a *sesshin,* a period of intense zazen meditation lasting several days. Every day, from four in the morning until nine at night, I worked in the kitchen. One time when the dishes came back from the meditation hall, I was disturbed to find two with some food left in them. Knowing that our practice forbids the waste of food, I wondered what had happened. I looked carefully and found in both dishes a vegetable fragment with a dead insect on it. I could easily imagine the two trainees spotting dead insects in their food and losing their appetites. Perplexed over whether or not to eat the food anyway, they would have felt deeply pained. Zen Master Dogen wrote in his *Tenzo Kyokun:* "First of all, check to see whether there are any insects, peas, rice-bran, or tiny stones in the rice, and if so, carefully winnow them out." Although I thought I had washed the vegetables thoroughly, two insects had escaped my notice.

During a lecture after the *sesshin,* I apologized for my carelessness. Then I told the following story. When I was a child, a man who taught the art of raising silkworms boarded at our temple. He told me about an incident that had occurred soon after he took up a new appointment as a teacher in Aichi Prefecture. The tea ceremony is very popular in that part of Japan. It is a district where people use the ceremonial powdered green tea as readily as people drink ordinary tea in other parts of the country.

One very hot day in midsummer, feeling extremely thirsty, he stopped at a farmhouse and asked for a cup of tea. In Aichi Prefecture, even an ordinary farmhouse has a tea ceremony room. In fact, the old man at that particular farm happened to be a fine practitioner. He misinterpreted the teacher's request, and, asking him to wait a moment, he went inside, changed his clothes, and prepared the tea ceremony room. The teacher had no knowledge of the tea ceremony and was at a loss as to what to do. He simply drank the bowl of tea that the old man had so carefully prepared for him and then fled, thoroughly disconcerted.

What comes next is important. After that incident, the old man told the neighbors: ''That teacher is such a connoisseur of the tea ceremony that I thought it better not to serve him at all than to do him the discourtesy of performing it unsatisfactorily.'' An ordinary person might have told everyone that the teacher had no appreciation of the tea ceremony. But the old man felt he had misunderstood the teacher and blamed himself for having put him in an embarrassing position. Hoping the teacher would never have to go through such an experience again, the old man made up a story and spread it throughout the community. This is the way of a true practitioner of tea.

The sixteenth-century tea master Sen no Rikyu taught: "Be the host at one with the heart of the guest; be the guest at one with the heart of the host. . . . The carelessness of the guest becomes the carelessness of the host. The carelessness of the host becomes the carelessness of the guest." Needless to say, an insect or the like in a dish indicates a serious shortcoming on the part of the cook. However, a guest who leaves food on his plate because there is a bug in it lacks consideration.

It is difficult to put oneself in another's place. When we feel we should express sympathy to someone who is ill or has lost possessions in a fire, for example, a visit would be appropriate. But do we really go in a spirit of sympathy? Or do we go because we feel obliged to do so? If the latter is the case, then our visit may serve only to tire the person.

When I was in the hospital several years ago, I was afraid that having visitors would tire me, so I entered the hospital almost in secret. Even so, the news spread and people came. While I was grateful that they had taken the trouble to come in the August heat, their visits wore me out completely. One visitor, however, was markedly different from the others. She was a housewife and arrived in her apron, saying, "Abbess, let me do your laundry for you. Shall I rub your back?"

In *Tenzo Kyokun,* Zen Master Dogen quoted injunctions to be considerate even toward things: "Zen Master Jen Yung of Pao-ning said, 'Use the property and possessions of the community as carefully as if they were your own eyes.' " "There is an old saying that goes, 'See the pot as your own head; see the water as your lifeblood.' " "When you handle water, rice, or anything else, you must have the affectionate and caring concern of a parent raising a child." He called this attitude Parental Mind.

Magnanimous Mind

The Zen term *kanshiketsu* literally means "shit-stick." In China, a monk calling on Zen Master Yüen-men (d. 949) asked, "What is a buddha?" Yüen-men replied, "A dried shit-stick."

When the abbot or any of the teachers is away from a temple for a week or so, the novices think nothing of it. But if there were no toilet paper, they would quickly feel its absence. Shit-sticks, which were used in former days for the same purpose, could be washed and used any number of times. Shit-sticks become dirty to clean us. If these are not buddhas, what is? Out of gratitude for them, I recognize the shit-stick as a buddha. And this makes me wonder whether, if I were given a filthy task, I would be able to tackle it with the same attitude that I would deal with any of the duties of abbess. Would I happily take pride in it? I would probably complain, compare it unfavorably with other work, and be tormented by a feeling of inferiority.

Zen Master Kosho Uchiyama said, "Violets are violets. Roses are roses. Budding, blossoming, fading, aging, becoming diseased—all are stages. As we go through these stages ourselves, let us bloom and grace the present moment of eternity." In the mundane world there are countless roles and degrees of status. In the world of truth, the world of the Buddha, however, nothing is useless. Everything is equally important, irreplaceable, and precious. Nothing is inessential. If there were no toilet paper, we would not get through the day. If a garbage truck did not come around once in a while, we would be in serious trouble. Getting smeared with excrement or covered with dirt is the ultimate form of buddhahood. We may think we understand this, but when it is our turn to get our hands dirty, we end up complaining.

Yoshio Toi, the Buddhist monk, frequently gave a talk entitled "Bowing to the Soles of People's Feet." On one occasion another lecturer approached him afterward, bowed to the soles of his feet, and began massaging them, saying, "Reverend Toi, when you return home, please bow to the soles of your wife's feet and massage them like this."

Reverend Toi did so and later told us his thoughts about the experience. He said: "It had been over twenty years since we were married, and yet this was the first time I had ever seen the soles of my wife's feet. I was shocked to find how rough and misshapen they were. Then it came to me. My wife, who was born in a city temple, undoubtedly had much nicer feet when she first came to my temple as a young bride. In my place, she would always inspect the fields, function as the caretaker of the temple, and go out on any errands. She shouldered all the rough work at our poor temple up in the mountains, tilling the fields and gardens, carrying heavy bags on her back. Her feet had suffered as she trudged among the rocks and tree roots on mountain paths. Realizing the truth of this, I bowed to them and massaged them in earnest.''

Have we ever seriously examined, bowed to, or appreciated in any way the soles of our feet, which have done all the work of sustaining the body, always bearing the brunt of our walking? Even if we did, would we truly discover their worth without comparing them to other parts of the body, and enjoy work that requires us to assume a role similar to the soles of our feet? They support the whole body. If they are not a buddha, what is? But even this kind of discernment is delusion. True commitment to one's role has no room for thoughts like these.

Zen Master Dogen says in *Tenzo Kyokun:* "When making a soup with ordinary greens, do not be carried away by feelings of dislike towards them nor regard them lightly; neither jump for joy simply because you have been given ingredients of superior quality to make a special dish.'' He reprimanded those who would scorn a simple vegetable soup and make a full effort only for a special feast, that is, those whose speech and attitude depend on the people or materials involved. In the last part of the text, concerning the Three Minds, he wrote, "Magnanimous Mind is like a mountain, stable and impartial. Exemplifying the ocean, it is tolerant and views everything from the broadest perspective. Having a Magnanimous Mind means being without prejudice and refusing to take sides." To do anything that Buddhist practice requires, happily and with concentrated devotion, without entertaining likes or dislikes—whether it involves cleaning shit-sticks, performing an abbess's duties, making a simple vegetable soup, or preparing a great feast—this can be called Magnanimous Mind.

High Things in High Places; Low Things in Low Places

I recall another story about shit-sticks. Several years ago, soon after I returned from a pilgrimage to the Buddhist holy places in India, I talked with a doctor about how I had been inconvenienced by the shortage of restroom facilities. The doctor, who had served in Burma and Thailand during the Second World War, recalled his own experiences:

"None but upper-class families used toilets. Ordinary people made do with the outdoors. Buddhist monks are greatly respected there, so monks and doctors—people of high status—were treated to the use of toilet facilities. The first time I stepped inside one, I noticed something like a chopstick-holder in one corner. In it were shiny, flat, black sticks like chopsticks. In another corner were more sticks, but these had something stuck on them. At first I couldn't figure out what they were, but finally I realized that they were a substitute for toilet paper. Later they were gathered, washed, and reused. Japanese soldiers mistook them for chopsticks, you know. Chopsticks are not readily available in these countries, so they were delighted to find some and would carry them away."

Reeling with laughter, I understood that the tale of the shit-sticks still has meaning. No matter how valuable shit-sticks may be, or how indispensable, we would certainly be in trouble if they were confused with chopsticks. The ancients teach us this in beautiful language: "Spring is neither high nor low. The flowering branches are naturally long or short."

Spring comes to all, equally. It does not come quickly because someone wants it to, or slowly to one who wishes for delay. Spring arrives for everyone in the same fashion. In the sunlight, violets are violets, cherry blossoms are cherry blossoms. Some of the flowering stems or branches are short and others are long. Each blooms with a flower unique to it.

In *Tenzo Kyokun,* Dogen says: "Put those things that naturally go in a high place onto a high place, and those that would be most stable in a low place onto a low place; things that naturally belong in a high place settle best in a high place, while those which belong in a low place find their greatest stability there.'' Wooden rice containers and rice scoops, and anything else, should be placed where they belong. And never handle anything roughly, being careful only of expensive items and throwing cheap ones around. It is taught that all things in heaven and earth should be carefully put in place, one by one, with sincerity.

Savor Each Moment in Life

The taxi driver was grumbling: ''This kind of work is pretty worthless, and I know it's all I'll ever do with my life.''

Quite spontaneously I retorted, ''Your job is certainly not worthless. You become both arms and legs for people, carrying them where they need to go. People like myself could never manage without you. An understanding driver always goes as close to the speed limit as he can to get me to my destination on time. Even though I'm forever going about here and there, I never bother to take an umbrella with me. The driver kindly shields me from the rain, taking me right up to the place I want to go. He also helps me to carry my bags, because I always walk about with as much hand luggage as a person leaving on a trip. And whereas I have no natural sense of direction, the taxi driver will find his way through winding lanes, asking directions where necessary. Taxi drivers safely deliver home those who miss the last train because their meeting was delayed or because they were out drinking too late. When a person has to get to a hospital suddenly, a taxi can be a lifesaver. When no one else can take you where you have to go, because everyone is on holiday or it's the dead of night, one can always rely on the taxi driver. Don't you agree that this is wonderful work after all?''

As I had him taking me quite a distance, I continued: ''I seriously believe that there is not one worthless thing, not a single useless thing in the whole world. The other day, I gave a lecture at a company that manufactures watches and calculators. When the lecture was over, the company president took me on a tour of the factory, and I was really impressed. I watched parts being assembled that can be seen only with a microscope, and on a conveyor belt at that. If one of those parts being poked around by the point of a needle is out of place to the tiniest extent, the entire watch, the entire calculator, will be out of sync, or could stop altogether. I felt very keenly how each single part shouldered the work of the entire piece.

''And I thought that one household, or, to widen the image a bit, a society or country, or, to widen the image even further, heaven and earth and even the universe itself function in the very same way as one of these watches. Most people see

things in terms of superior and inferior, higher
and lower values. But seen from the standpoint of
truth, there are neither superior nor inferior,
neither higher nor lower values. No matter where
you begin, the entire family, the entire society, the
entire universe is fully in place at every single
point. The perspective alters quite dramatically if
we are alert enough to see the difference between
the biased view that our work is merely one
trifling, mechanical part, and the attitude that,
whatever we do, it shoulders all heaven and earth,
all past, present, and future.

"When Shakyamuni Buddha was born, he
pointed to heaven with one hand and to earth with
another. You might have heard that he said, 'I
alone am honored, in heaven and on earth.' He
meant that all sentient beings have value. No matter what person, what kind of work, what flower or
bird, they have all received the great gift of life
from heaven and earth, whether they realize it or
not."

I suppose it was presumptuous to talk about
these things to the driver for so long, but he
listened seriously. I was glad to hear him say,
"Well, what you've said gives me hope. I'll try
and do my best."

Zen Master Hsüeh-tou (980–1052) said:

> One, seven, three, five—
> The truth you search for cannot be grasped.
> As night advances, a bright moon
>   illuminates the whole ocean;

> The dragon's jewels are found in every wave.
> Looking for the moon, it is here,
>   in this wave, in the next.

"One, seven, three, five" is supposed to suggest life's unpredictability. Anything can happen. Life does not follow a set pattern. If we wonder where truth is hidden or whether we can find worthwhile work, we will restlessly look beyond ourselves. But just as the moonlight glitters on the crest of every wave, every thing and every person is important and has his or her own splendor. Not a single thing is insignificant. That is what Zen Master Dogen taught in *Tenzo Kyokun* and *Fushuku Hampo* (Table Manners for Zen Monks), and particularly in the sections entitled "Washing the Face" and "Rules for the Lavatory" in *Shobo-genzo*.

Viewing the Changes of the Seasons as a Whole

It was summertime. I and about twenty of my former tea ceremony pupils from when I had lived in Tokyo gathered at a certain place in the Japan Alps, in Nagano Prefecture. Carrying only the most necessary tea ceremony utensils, we hiked up to the plateau at the source of the Azusa River and enjoyed an outdoor tea ceremony there. After that we pushed on to Myojin Pond.

It was very refreshing to be walking in the mountains. Even as we hurried along the mountain path, we did not perspire. Our eyes drank in the sight of green that knew nothing of smog. The wind brought us the songs of many kinds of birds. We could see the Azusa River flowing behind the larch and birch trees, with the bright summer sunlight dancing on the crest of each ripple. The pebbles were clearly visible at the bottom of the river. Duckweed quivered in the current. Everything looked as though we could reach out and touch it. Within the shadow of the rocks grew trilliums and rock moss, wet from the river spray. The August sky was clear as far as one could see. White clouds floated by, softening the severe outline of the soaring mountain peaks.

I forgot about Myojin Pond and just enjoyed the scenery as it unfolded, calling out in my joy at the sight of the wild grasses and flowers. Suddenly someone in our group interrupted my reverie: "Aren't we at Myojin Pond yet? It's far, isn't it? I'm already tired out." Whenever we met a person coming back along the same path, she asked, "How much further is there to go?" It made me recall some lines from Hermann Hesse's "The Secret Art of Travel":

> To the eyes only looking hurriedly to the goal,
> The sweetness of roaming cannot be savored.
> Forests and streams and all of the magnificent
>   spectacles waiting along the way
> Remain closed off.

The secret of traveling lies in savoring the things along the way. If you are in a hurry to reach your goal, you miss seeing the forests and the streams and the momentary, unblemished twinkling of the stars. I savored Hesse's poem anew and thought to myself that it was just the same with life. Enjoying each step of the way means making it a destination in itself. We should have thought of Myojin Pond only as a point on the compass. Our real goal was what lay immediately ahead. In life, we never know what is going to happen. Last year on this mountain peak, local high school students were in serious danger when they were caught in a thunderstorm. Sometimes people fall ill while climbing. If you have a goal like Myojin Pond and strain yourself to reach it, has your whole effort been wasted if you fall by the wayside? No. If we savor each step toward our destination as an experience never to be repeated, then we will have learned a way of walking in which any stopping place is good.

What does it mean to enjoy ourselves along the way in life's journey? There are times when we fail at work we had seriously grappled with, are misunderstood, or feel surrounded by enemies. Then again, there are other times when we are so ecstatic we could be riding a rainbow to paradise. There are times when we stand at the edge of the precipice of losing a husband, wife, or a child. There is the downhill plunge of a terminal illness, or of not having enough to eat. The journey with constant changes of scenery is the most interesting. It is the same with life's journey. It is important not to be swayed by fortune; instead, we must learn to look at the scenery and enjoy it each step of the way.

In his *Tenzo Kyokun,* Zen Master Dogen says, "Magnanimous Mind is like a mountain, stable and impartial. Exemplifying the ocean, it is tolerant and views everything from the broadest perspective. Having a Magnanimous Mind means being without prejudice and refusing to take sides. When carrying something that weighs an ounce, do not think of it as light, and, likewise, when you have to carry fifty pounds, do not think of it as heavy. Do not get carried away by the sounds of spring, nor become heavy-hearted upon seeing the colors of fall. View the changes of the seasons as a whole, and weigh the relativeness of light and heavy from a broad perspective."

"The sounds of spring" symbolizes good fortune, and "the colors of fall" bad fortune. When we meet with misfortune, we often get upset and try to escape, fettering ourselves, and end up losing heart. On the other hand, good fortune can be intoxicating. We should view fortune like the changes of the seasons: as a whole. That is, we should welcome good and bad as one, not letting ourselves be shaken by either. Nature and the real journey of life go on developing regardless of our mundane personal thoughts and worries.

When we throw off the petty self and quietly give ourselves body and soul into nature's keeping, then the fragrance of the plum blossom enduring the freezing wind, the throb of new life hidden in the springtime mud, and the welcoming voice of the plants and trees making merry in the thunder and rain are all able to reach us.

The Gift of a Smiling Face

> With just your being there,
> The atmosphere somehow brightens.
> With just your being there,
> Everyone feels at ease.
> I yearn to be just like you.

This is my favorite poem by the calligrapher Mitsuo Aida. It means that when we are with other people, even if we cannot think of anything clever to say, we should try by our very presence to brighten the surroundings and make everyone comfortable. I am incredibly happy when I come across a person who does that. I gaze at him or her lovingly and wish I could do the same. On the other hand, some people who enter a room cast a pall. When I meet that kind of person, I feel as if I am seeing my bad side and am saddened. I am made to reflect on whether I, too, make others depressed or uneasy.

There is a story I cannot forget, even though it took place quite some time ago. I heard it from the essayist Toru Matsui, about a young Christian woman named Reiko Kitahara, the daughter of a professor.

It happened in a corner of downtown Tokyo

THE GIFT OF A SMILING FACE 103

that had been bombed to rubble during the Second
World War. A shantytown called Ant Town had
sprung up there, where ragpickers lived. Reiko
went to live there. She assembled the local children, who were too poor to go to school, and became their teacher. Often going without sleep,
she also looked after the sick and elderly who lived
alone. Every morning, several hundred ragpickers
would go out, pulling their rattling wooden carts
behind them. She would always see them off with a
bright smile, saying, "Have a good day!" In the
evening, no matter how late the hour, she would
always welcome them back with a smile, saying,
"You must be tired." The mere sight of her
gentle, innocent smile made these rough men,
who had drifted to Ant Town in the postwar
chaos, completely forget their weariness. Thus
Reiko came to be idolized as the Blessed Virgin of
Ant Town.

Eventually she came down with tuberculosis.
Although people urged her to go back to her
parents' home to recover, she said, "Let me die
here." In a corner of a hovel, where a cold wind
blew in through the cracks, she lay on a tattered
mattress, taking neither medicine nor any special
nourishment. She left the world while still young,
in her twenties. After her death, a small notebook
was found under her pillow. She had taken it out
from time to time as she lay on her sickbed.
Wondering if something important was written in
it, Matsui opened it and found just one sentence:
"Aren't you forgetting to smile right now?" It

seems that even as she lay with a high fever, she did not lose her smile. Yet she was, after all, no saint, but an ordinary human being. Her cruel illness must sometimes have made her want to cry, despite her wish to spare others. At such times, she must have pulled out that notebook and struggled to ask herself that question.

To be always smiling seems a small thing, but actually it is hard. Anyone can smile when it suits him. But to be able to smile at any time—to be able to smile even when it does not suit us—is no easy task. In the long run, few people can see themselves for what they really are. But when we look in the mirror, we see the face others are going to see. Someone else will be made uncomfortable if we look irritable or angry. Whatever our mood, we should try not to inflict it on others, even if we think that is the way we are and it cannot be helped. We should take responsibility for ourselves and take proper care of ourselves, keeping our face from looking unpleasant and adding to the world's unpleasantness.

Shakyamuni Buddha's list of the "Seven Offerings That Cost Nothing" includes a smiling face. He wished that everyone would smile and accept all other people in the way that a mother smiles on her children and opens her arms to embrace them.

Looking Hard at Life

The well-known haiku poet Kobayashi Issa (1763–

1827) lived in the Shinshu area of Nagano Prefecture. His beloved wife died young, leaving behind a little child. He wrote the following poem as he looked, weeping, at the child on the day of the first Bon Festival after his wife's death. (The Bon Festival marks the time when spirits of the dead are believed to return to visit their former homes in this world.)

> The baby left behind murmurs,
> "Mama's coming,"
> And claps its hands.

Shortly afterward, the infant followed its mother in death, and Issa wrote:

> Hey, pretty pink flowers!
> All around is Jizo Bodhisattva,
> Behind and before.

Jizo is the patron of children and guides children who die to the next world, so Issa invoked his protection.

The term *bon* derives from the Sanskrit *ullambana*. It means rescue from the torment of hanging upside down in hell. The Bon Festival originates in the story of Moggallana saving his mother from one of the Buddhist hells, the realm of hungry spirits, where she was hanging upside down. A major disciple of the Buddha, Moggallana was known for his supernatural powers. After his mother died, he had a vision of her in that realm. He asked the Buddha how she could be saved, and the Buddha said that if Moggallana gave alms to fellow monks, he would earn merit that would be transferred to his mother, thus liberating her. This story teaches the importance of filial piety and the transfer of merit to ancestors.

In relation to our ancestors, we are like the apex of a pyramid. The levels of the pyramid ever widening toward its base represent past generations of ancestors. Our present existence is the sum of all they did, and we are the starting point for our descendants. All that our ancestors did reflects on us, and all that we do reflects on both our ancestors and our descendants. If we commit evil, we leave an indelible stain on the souls of both our ancestors and our descendants.

One's life is not entirely one's own; it contains the past and conceives the future, and should therefore be lived with great care. This is the teaching of the Bon Festival. The Buddha warned that those who forget it and lead self-centered lives are destined for the torment of hanging upside down in the realm of hungry spirits.

The Tale of a Female Demon

Every year, six or seven of my tea ceremony pupils, all of whom are women, marry, and five or six of these become mothers. Since I have a very poor memory, I have to make a point of remembering their children's names. Sometimes late at night I get a telephone call from the family of a former pupil with the news that she has given birth to a healthy baby, and they tell me its name. I am always as happy as if I were the mother. One former pupil wrote me, "When my child is old enough to understand, we would like to visit you at the temple to hear one of your lectures on the Buddha. I hope my child will forge a bond with the Buddha." Sometimes they come to see me on their way to a Shinto shrine with their newborn baby, where they will offer thanks for the blessing of the birth. Or they come with two children, carrying the younger one on their back and leading the older by the hand. Sometimes I cannot resist taking the younger one and holding it in my arms for a few moments.

While these women were my pupils, and even as they went off to marry, they seemed to have the innocent faces of young children. But when they came to visit me after a year of marriage, bringing their first child, I marveled at how mature they looked. Motherhood had matured them. It really seemed that they had passed through so many levels all at one time. They would change their baby's diapers and rejoice that it was healthy. If the baby would not swallow some food, they would put it into their own mouth first. Who but a mother would do these things? For a mother, a child is not something outside herself. In fact, the child might be even more important to her than her own body.

I also heard former pupils express gratitude toward their own mothers for having raised them. Now, with children of their own, they knew for the first time what a debt they owed their mothers. They did not talk about this emotionally, but I knew they spoke from the heart. I was much moved in discovering this beautiful relationship between mothers and daughters. I hoped that they would extend this love of theirs for their children and their own mothers to all people.

If one wanted a living example of the love of the buddhas in this world, one might picture a loving mother caring for her child. A mother's love is like a buddha's. On the other hand, it is partly animal instinct.

The Russian novelist and poet Ivan Turgenev describes the behavior of some sparrows in one of his books. A baby sparrow had fallen from the nest in a strong wind, and a hunting dog approached. The parents hurled themselves at the dog. They were willing to sacrifice themselves to save their baby. Turgenev intended to show that love is stronger than death, or even the fear of death.

A Buddhist sutra tells of a female demon named Hariti, who married and had lots of children. But in her wickedness she abducted and murdered children in Rajagriha, the capital of Magadha. The townspeople grew terrified, bolted their doors even in the daytime, and rarely went out. The Buddha was deeply grieved over this, and one morning, after gathering alms in the city, he went to Hariti's house. She was out, but her youngest child was playing there alone. The Buddha used his supernatural powers to hide the child in the bottom of his begging bowl. Then he left without anyone seeing him. When Hariti returned and saw that her beloved child was gone, she screamed and cried. Then she searched everywhere for the child, in the mountains, the fields, and all the surrounding towns and villages. When the child was nowhere to be found, she went and prostrated herself before the Buddha, saying, "I cannot find my youngest child anywhere and am about to lose my mind. Please have mercy on me and let me see my baby."

The Buddha just asked her quietly, "How many children do you have?" Hariti answered that she had many, and he admonished her, "Hariti! If you are so sad and tormented by the loss of just one of your many children, think of the sorrow of all those mothers who have lost their only child because of you!"

Hariti became aware for the first time of the awfulness of her crimes, and she cried as though her world were coming to an end. But at last she pulled herself together and repented before the Buddha, taking refuge in his teachings. He restored her beloved child to her, and she was known forever after as the guardian goddess of children.

That story has particular significance for mothers today. With the fierce competition in Japan to get into the best universities, there is the type of applicant who is happy if a fellow applicant is too sick to take the entrance examination, eliminating

at least one competitor. Mothers of these appli-
cants are known as "education mamas," and
they do anything to get their child into a good
university. They have even been known to steal
copies of exams. It is a world of "eat or be
eaten." These women are the modern version of
the female demon.

For better or for worse, the sight of a mother doing everything she can for her child is very
beautiful. If her love is unenlightened, however, it
differs from the Buddha's love. Sad to say, it is
only when people are deprived of someone or
something they love that they come to understand
its value, and the joy and sadness of loving.

People with stomach trouble are made aware of
their stomachs and learn to appreciate a strong
stomach. They are likely to sympathize with other
people who have stomach trouble. People who are
hurt, sad, or tormented can easily sympathize with
others. What converted Hariti from a female
demon who abducted and murdered children to a
loving guardian goddess of children was her experience of suffering what she had made others
suffer. The anguish that she went through on ac-
count of her missing child awakened her to a
deeper, selfless love.

I hope and pray that each of my students who
bring their children to meet me will learn from the
love they have for their children a deeper, broader
kind of love that they can extend to everyone they
meet.

A Mother's Daily Conduct

"This morning I had a dream about my mother. In the dream she said, 'Your right shoulder is sticking out from under the covers.' My white-haired mother, over eighty years old, moved around my bed, patting down the quilt. I lost her twenty-seven years ago. I come from the island of Shikoku, which has a mild climate, so it seems cold to me here in the Japan Alps. When I think of her following me in a dream all the way here, taking care of me so that I won't catch cold, I am deeply moved."

At this point the voice of Sumita Oyama, a haiku poet from Matsuyama in Shikoku, faltered, but soon he was able to continue.

"I have always been proud of my mother. The housewife in a large farming family, she had no formal education. She told me that, from the day she knew I was in her womb until the day I was born, she went every day to a little temple dedicated to Kannon, the bodhisattva of mercy, just outside the village. It seemed appropriate, then, that I should have been born on Kannon's Festival Day. My mother's love did not start at my birth, but from the time she first knew that she was carrying me. My education also began in the womb. During pregnancy, only the mother is in close contact with the child. Throughout this time, fortunately, I was protected and guided by Kannon Bodhisattva because of my mother's frequent visits to the temple. And after I was born, she often took me there.

"In spite of being raised in this way, I was not able to be at peace with myself, either religiously or philosophically, until past the age of thirty. It was when I was about thirty-four or -five years old that I truly understood my mother's love, which seemed to reflect the Buddha's mind. Around that time, I was working in telecommunications in Hiroshima, where I was in charge of training employees. One day a telegram arrived from home reading, 'MOTHER UNCONSCIOUS. RETURN AS SOON AS POSSIBLE.' There is no news more painful to someone away from home. I entrusted my work to several of the others there, and by the time I finally set out for home, it was late at night. The last train had already gone, and I had to walk to the ferry. On the Shikoku side I walked on and on through the night. Just as dawn broke, I finally arrived at the back gate of our house. I noticed some small purple flowers that had fallen in a light rain from the paulownia tree. Then I saw our old family doctor coming out of the house, walking on the fallen flowers.

" 'How is my mother?' I asked agitatedly.

" 'She collapsed from a stroke. I treated her immediately, but so far she hasn't regained consciousness. Hurry in and see her.'

"I sat down beside her pillow. No matter how many times I called her, there was no answer, just the eerie, deep snoring sound she made. My father was constantly watching over her. He told me not to touch her. Wanting to be as close to her as I could, I drew near and gazed at her. The warmth of her feverish body wafted over me. What came to mind at that moment were all the times I had been contrary to her and caused her pain. Without eating or sleeping, I prayed by her side, waiting for her to open her eyes.

"The following night, as the wall clock struck nine, my mother regained consciousness. When she saw me lying there beside her, she called to my wife, who was now also there with us, and said in a faltering voice, 'Sumita's shoulder . . . seems to be . . . sticking out . . . from . . . under the quilt. He mustn't . . . catch cold, so please . . . go . . . get another . . . quilt.' When I heard that, it wrenched my guts and I cried out. Feeling embarrassed with so many people in the room, I covered my head with the quilt and stifled the sound of my sobs.

"The question had been, would my mother, who had collapsed and slept through an entire day and night, revive again or die without ever awakening? But when she did at last awake, this mother of mine was not thinking of her own illness but only worrying about me, who was as healthy as could be. When I realized her deep and selfless love for me, everything became resolved. From that moment forward, at long last, I knew how I would live my life. If I had not been at my mother's side at that time or had that experience, I might have lived out my days never having had the great fortune of really understanding her love for me. It saddens me to think of her illness, but it was through her deep and selfless love that I realized the quality of the Buddha's compassion. I am grateful for her illness as a revelation of the Buddha's intention for me.''

It was in 1969 that Mr. Oyama shared these memories of his mother. Of the more than one hundred people listening, all were close to tears. We all thought of our own mothers. Some may have thought that they, like Mr. Oyama, had good mothers. Others may have felt regret at having given their mothers a hard time. Others were miserable because they could not respect their mothers. All sorts of people with all sorts of memories heard this talk.

It is the mother whom the infant accepts with its pure body and mind when it comes into the world. The one who is always physically closest to the infant during the most important period of growth is also the mother. There is a Japanese proverb that says, ''What is instilled by the age of three is remembered to the age of a hundred.'' And it is primarily the mother who instills what her child learns up to three years of age. A cheerful mother raises a cheerful child; a complaining mother raises a complaining child; and a mother who is always angry will raise a short-tempered child.

The Buddhist scholar and priest Haya Akegarasu wrote, ''There are one billion mothers for one billion people, but no mother is better than my mother.'' Even if a mother has no formal education or even if she is nothing special to look at, she should try to be the kind of mother about whom her child would say, "No mother is better than my mother." If we think an infant cannot understand anything at all because it has just been born, that is a great mistake. Each word from an unconcerned mother, each inattentive movement, is absorbed by the infant's body and mind like ink on unblemished blotting paper. Every act of ours, good or bad, will be an element in the infant's growth. With this in mind, a mother has to live her life with reverence.

A child raised by a good mother—say it is a boy—will grow up able to be a congenial and loving husband and a companionable father. If the child is a girl, she will make a pleasant mother and probably raise a child with a sunny disposition. The conduct of one mother with such a heart reveals itself in this way through ongoing generations. A mother's life is not confined to her alone. She is the starting point of life that unfolds into the infinite future. The opposite is also true. If, for example, a cup of dirty water is poured into the upper reaches of a river, it remains in the river all the way down and into the sea. Thinking of this, each mother must feel that she should continue trying to be the best mother in the world by being careful in thoughts, choice of words, and behavior.

My Two Teachers

"Master!" There are several people that I would

like to be allowed to call "Master," with all the love and respect I feel welling up from the bottom of my heart when I use that word. I have been able to come this far in my life only because I have had so many good teachers and friends, and I owe them a debt of gratitude.

If I had not met a certain person at a certain time, if I had not encountered this person's words at this moment, what kind of life would I be living today? Just to imagine it puts a lump in my throat. But we must remember that, even if a great master stands before us expounding the true teachings, if we do not aspire to the Way and pay no attention to him, no connection can be made and a teacher-disciple relationship cannot be formed. Whenever I remember that simple truth, I think about the two teachers who nurtured from the very beginning my aspiration to seek and practice the Way on my own.

I have had a long and deep connection with Buddhism. From the time I was carried in my mother's womb, it was planned that I would enter the priesthood. In the spring when I was five, I entered a temple called Muryo-ji in Nagano Prefecture, where my aunt, the old nun Shuzan, presided. I became the disciple of Senshu, the nun next in charge and a cousin of Shuzan. Shuzan took me directly to the Buddha Hall, where she sat me in front of the main Buddha statue while she talked to me:

"Take a good, long look at this Buddha. The thumb and forefinger on each hand form a circle, don't they?'' The statue was of Amida Buddha, who is always depicted in this way. ''No matter where you are, whether asleep or awake, or even if you completely forget about the Buddha, he is always watching over you. If you do something naughty when you think no one is looking, the circles made by his fingers will turn into triangles!''

Young and innocent as I was, I fully believed that. No matter what it was I did, I thought of the face and hands of that statue of Amida Buddha. Whenever I did something bad, or was lazy, or hurt someone's feelings by something I had said, I would worry about whether the circles formed by Amida Buddha's fingers had changed to triangles, and I would crawl up on the dark altar to take a look. His face was always smiling, his fingers joined in circles.

The words ''always watching over you'' are full of trust and promise. No matter how hard I tried, there were times when I was misunderstood, reproached, or felt hemmed in on all sides. It was at these times that I felt embraced by the warmth emanating from Amida Buddha's hands and did not feel alone. The words ''always watching over you'' are also rather awesome. Whenever I was carried away by the praises of people around me, it would suddenly come to me that Amida Buddha's fingers might be forming triangles.

My wish was that no matter how I appeared in the eyes of worldly people, I wanted to live my life in a way that Amida Buddha always approved of.

But although I often failed in that, I always found
peace of mind in thinking that Amida Buddha embraced me as I was.

As a child I learned the importance of living according to the Buddha's way of measuring things.
I also learned that a life interwoven with joy,
anger, sadness, and pleasure, by happiness and
unhappiness, is itself in the very palm of the Buddha's hand. I was able to receive these two
teachings in the very first stage of my life. I feel
that the years since have been spent confirming
those teachings through practice.

From the day I first passed through the temple
gate, I began to memorize the short sutras, such as
the Adoration of the Relics of Shakyamuni Buddha, and the Heart of Wisdom Sutra. By the time
I graduated from junior high school, I had learned
almost all of the sutras that were taught at training temples. Shuzan, while she was really a warm
person, was also strict. For 365 days of the year,
she never permitted me to sleep late. We got up
while it was still pitch dark outside to hold morning service for one hour. In the dead of winter the
temperature was no more than minus fifteen
degrees Celsius in the Buddha Hall of our mountain temple, and my small hands were completely
numb as I beat the wooden block in accompani-
ment to sutra recitation with all my might. There
was a set time each evening when I was taught the
sutras. No matter how cold it was, I had to leave
the vicinity of the heater, bow with my hands
placed neatly before me on the floor, and say

"Please teach me." Shuzan also left her warm place, and, sitting formally on her knees, she pointed to the Chinese characters with a stick and read them to me one by one. At such times Senshu would be doing needlework beside us. After the sutra-reading lessons, Senshu would often recall stories of the Zen masters.

When I was in primary school, on holidays I was allowed exactly an hour for play after lunch. One time when I was out playing, I lost track of time and returned an hour late. Shuzan poured a bucket of well water over my head and scolded me severely. Later, when I was in high school, I was not given any free time for study. The only time I had for study, even during final exams, was either during the four-mile walk to and from school, or when I should have been sleeping. I was told, "When people are told to study, they lose the desire to study. If they don't think they have time for study, they instead struggle to create it. Then they can really use what time they have very efficiently." The hard work I had to do never made me cry, but I sometimes shed tears over not having time for study. When picking weeds in the garden or mulberry leaves to feed the silkworms, even when I was in the bathroom, I secretly reviewed my English vocabulary flash cards. The challenge was to fit in as much as possible in the twenty-four hours of a day. That way of life became the foundation for the way I live now.

Yoshio Toi once said, "To make one hundred children out of a hundred hate to study, just bark

at them 'Study! Study!' from morning till night.''
These words made me think that I was lucky
to have been raised and educated by my two
teachers.

I was ordained in the spring of my sixteenth
year, filled with the dream of walking the supreme
path. After my years of training at Aichi Semmon
Niso-do (a training temple for female Soto Zen
priests), I went on to attend the school affiliated
with the Soto sect, Komazawa University in
Tokyo. For fifteen years, until the summer of my
thirtieth year, my two teachers were undemanding
and gave me time, allowing me to enjoy myself in
college.

Impelled by my youthful purity, an uncom-
promising will, and impatience, I searched for the
Way but was too quickly disappointed. I searched
again, and despaired. Every time I despaired, I
lamented the corruption I saw in Buddhist or-
ganizations and denounced the Buddhist clergy.
My two teachers, Shuzan and Senshu, took me severely to task. ''Just how great a person do you
think you are? Everybody has some good points. If
you don't have the modesty of heart to be able to
learn from any and everyone, what are you going
to do?'' Even now these words echo in my ears.
The fifteen years of my youth spent in vainly seeking the Way had been like following an endlessly
curving mountain road. In spite of that, I finally
made my path. With a new sense of admiration for
the profundity and splendor of the Way, I was able

to return to our mountain temple in search of spiritual growth.

From the summer that I returned to our temple, I began holding annual zazen retreats. Year by year the number of participants grew, and soon both bedding and places to sleep were all taken up. My two teachers gladly offered their bedding, and for their own beds spread out cushions in the closets. It was Senshu who always acted as chef in the kitchen, overseeing the food for what was originally a hundred guests and now had grown to over two hundred. In her late years she was troubled with cataracts, and her vision was greatly impaired. But she would say, "I am still able to fire up the bath," and so she fed the firewood into the bath furnace. At the end of the annual zazen retreat in the summer of 1974, in her ninety-fourth year, she said, "I will hang on until next summer, waiting for you all to return. Be sure and come again next year!" But this was to be her last summer, for she left us that December.

My two teachers did the thankless work in the background while, I, the disciple, never wet my hands, was never choked by smoke, but instead sat in front of the participants, explaining zazen and the Dharma. Wanting to repay my teachers in some way, although knowing those debts could never be fully repaid, one year I persuaded the other nuns at the training temple to let me do the cooking during the intense zazen retreats. From four in the morning until after nine at night, I worked alone in the kitchen, recalling what I owed my teachers. I pray that someday I, too, will be blessed with the opportunity to have disciples stand in front of people explaining zazen while I stay behind in the kitchen or in the fields for the whole day, just as my teachers did for me.

Improvement Should Begin with Oneself

> Look not at the faults of others,
> At what they have done or left undone;
> Rather, look at what you yourself
> Have done or left undone.
>
> (Dhammapada, verse 50)

"What they have done" means errors they have made. "What they have left undone" refers to their having neglected to do what they should have done. Instead of always looking at others, let us try asking "What about myself? Have I not failed to act according to the Buddhist teachings? Have I given in to an egocentric point of view? Haven't I been remiss in fulfilling my duties in the Way?"

If we are the slightest bit careless, we lose track of our own path and wander off into the speech and conduct of those "others." Every time we notice this in ourselves, we must earnestly remind ourselves not to look at the faults of others. We can see others, but we cannot see ourselves, as explained in the Dhammapada:

Others' faults are easily perceived,
But one's own are difficult to perceive;
A man winnows his neighbor's faults
     like chaff,
But his own faults he hides,
As a cheat hides the bad die from
     the gambler.

(Dhammapada, verse 252)

How can we change from always looking for weaknesses in others to being open to criticism of ourselves?

If you meet a man who tells you your faults,
Welcome it as if he were pointing out
     buried treasures, and heed him.
It will be better, not worse,
For those who heed him.

(Dhammapada, verse 76)

Everyone is happy to be praised. When it comes to having faults pointed out, it does not feel very good, even if we understand that someone is trying to be kind in doing so. Another person might start some malicious gossip, but will not say anything to our face. When it gets back to us, we get angry and say, "If he or she had only had the courage to tell me that to my face!" In fact, if they were to speak to us directly, we would not be able to accept their criticism after all. This is the sad truth of our egocentric selves. As I was thinking of this, I came across these words of Rennyo (1414–

99), the restorer and eighth abbot of the True Pure Land sect: "If something is difficult to tell me to my face, go and tell it to someone else as if it were malicious gossip. That way I will want to hear it and correct my faults." I was deeply impressed by this. With someone like Rennyo, even slander can be converted into the light of the buddhas. I would like to be capable of accepting any kind of criticism.

What should we do when we are in a position of having to caution others about weaknesses and mistakes? Zen Master Dogen's teacher in China, Ju-ching (1163–1228), in order to spur on the monks, would take off one of his shoes and strike them with it, rebuking them with harsh words. The monks gladly accepted this treatment. This is written in the *Shobo-genzo Zuimonki.*

Zen Master Ju-ching once entered the meditation hall and confessed with tears in his eyes, "I am chief priest and the teacher of all of you in order to help you rid yourselves of all delusions and practice the Buddha's Way. This means that I sometimes have to scold you with harsh words or beat you with a bamboo stick. These are things no one should have to do, but it's up to me to do them on the Buddha's behalf so that your discipline will bear fruit. Brothers, have the compassion to forgive me, and accept my correction."

Because he rebuked them in an earnest and humble way, praying with a compassionate heart that they might awaken to the true teachings, Ju-ching was praised by the monks for striking them.

If this were not the Buddha's love, parental love, and selfless love, that kind of admonition would be inconceivable.

Fear of Criticism Is Unworthy

If Shakyamuni Buddha can be compared to the sun, then transmitting the light of the sun to people should be the role of Buddhist priests. But the priests of today seem like black clouds covering the sun. I would like to be a cloud just to play around the sun, to decorate the sun, but without realizing it I would also veil the sun if I remained as I am. And I would lose track of my true self in the arrogance of consciously trying to transmit the sun's rays. I am capable of being such a person. With just this one life to live, we go off to conquer the world and end up by being taken in. I have not wished to live that kind of life, and what helped support me in my youthful days of seeking, getting lost, and then seeking again was Shakyamuni's reply to Atula in verses 227 and 228 of the Dhammapada.

One day a youth named Atula went to see Shakyamuni Buddha. Atula had been upset over rumors about himself. After the Buddha listened carefully to everything Atula had to say, these were his words of counsel, as quoted in the Dhammapada:

"This is an old saying, Atula, it is not a saying of today: They blame the man who is silent, they blame the man who speaks too much, and they blame the man who speaks too little. No man can escape blame in this world.

"There never was, there never will be, nor is there now, a man whom men always blame, nor a man whom they always praise."

Shakyamuni meant that such things have happened since ancient times. They are not things that have begun recently. If a person keeps silent, others will complain that he is tight-lipped. If he speaks a little, there are again those who will criticize. Speaking much, he will be criticized for being over-talkative. No matter what he does, it is the nature of people to criticize. People who have only known criticism or only known praise have never existed, never will exist, and certainly do not exist now.

What wins praise from some people provokes criticism from others. This is a common, everyday occurrence. Feeling at all times the eyes of the Buddha upon me, I have aspired to live with those great eyes as my guide, rather than simply living in a way that does not draw irresponsible public criticism.

Along with Shakyamuni's words to Atula are others that have helped me in my self-discipline, such as those in *Shobo-genzo Zuimonki,* in which Dogen is quoted as saying, "If you are to be shamed, be shamed by a man of clear insight." One must experience shame. However, the person who shames us, and why, is the important thing. According to an old adage, "One ashamed of not meeting worldly standards thinks in a worldly way.''

When a mother scolds her child, she should be careful. Mothers often tell their children, ''If you do that, other people will laugh at you.'' But this way of scolding brings certain failure. It is dreadful to influence small children this way. Their minds are at an early stage of development, so their standards of behavior and even their morals will be subtly and gradually shaped by others' praise or blame.

One more problem with this way of scolding is that the child may feel it is all right to do something bad as long as it is not discovered. The point is whether the acts themselves are good or evil, not whether others will find out and praise or blame. Whether others praise or fail to notice, we must do nothing unworthy or contrary to the Way. Whether others blame or misunderstand, we must do things that are worthy and consistent with the Way. No matter what others say, we should come to a decision after asking in our heart for guidance from the Buddha. Parents must themselves live with this resolute attitude. And when they scold their children, I hope they will follow this philosophy.

Reading Mother's Unwritten Scripture

On the sun-warmed paper doors, a silhouette of forsythia just starting to bloom trembled in the wind. Sitting in front of the paper doors, I felt my back grow warmer and warmer, making me comfortably sleepy. I was enjoying a bowl of frothy green tea and listening to the soft murmur of the wind in the pines. My friend, seated next to me, suddenly said, "These days, it's strange even to me how awfully forgetful I am becoming. I guess I am not as sharp as I used to be. I try to really pay attention to the books I read, but nothing seems to stay in my head. Although as classmates we both had the same start, you have been in a position to use your head. With all your continuing efforts you have published some splendid books, gone here and there to give lectures—leading a really worthwhile life. Compared with that, my life has been taken up with farming and raising children. Not using my head much must be the reason that I have become so stupid. Even though we were in school together, our ways of life have certainly brought about different results, haven't they?"

I felt her lonely regret reverberate through what she was saying. This friend, far superior to me intellectually, could have become a university professor had she chosen an academic career. But being an only daughter, she had to marry, maintain the family line, and take over the farm, and was not allowed to go beyond high school. She could not help telling me now that when she realized that her whole life would consist of farming and child-rearing, she felt something like an empty wind pass through her heart. It struck home to me, quite painfully, what she meant. I replied with emphasis, "People on television or the radio or who write for newspapers or magazines may seem important, but there's nothing special about them. Since I happen to be blessed with this way of life, I simply do the best I can. In my work I can erase or rewrite. But farming and raising children allow no such corrections. Each 'sentence' that you make has to be complete and is for all time. Couldn't you say that you have been writing your sentences with your body and mind?

"Even though children may for a time resist the way their parents raise them, in the long run they will follow the pattern of their upbringing. Each word and each phrase they read now they will live later, without omitting anything that has been written by their parents' actions. You've been writing your one and only precious 'book' with your very life, and still continue to do so even now. Haven't you, then, lived a life that's as good as anyone else's?"

My friend's face began to radiate happiness. To give an example of children who read now, and later on live by, each word and phrase of their parents' actions, I went on to talk about my childhood:

"Father spent the last fifteen years of his life ill in bed. I was born about seven years before he died. My parents decided that I should become a nun. When I was five I was sent away from home to live in a temple, so I hardly remember my mother's way of life. Father died at the age of fifty-two. The only image I have is of him always lying down. A few days before his death a telegram came to the temple saying his life was in danger, and I was taken home. I stayed several days. What I saw of my mother in that short period has given me encouragement and support throughout my life.

"Around that time, my eighty-year-old grandmother was also bedridden from old age and infirmity. While caring for both my father and grandmother, Mother also bore the burden of farmwork and raising my elder brother and sister.

"She was thin as a rail and seemed to be always hurrying about. She had to make the rice cakes alone, a job that normally required several people: to steam the rice on a stove, which had to be fed with wood and straw; to pound the steamed rice with a heavy pestle; to roll layers of it to the right thickness; and from these to make the small round cakes. She took it for granted that she had to do the work alone and never complained. She just worked hard. When my father felt worse, he would often call her to his bedside. Since it would have been impossible for her to run the household if she had had to sit beside him all the time, when he was worse she would quickly pick some vegetables in the field and cook or pickle them in the kitchen, where she could hear him. After struggling with illness for fifteen years, my father left this world only two months after my grandmother. Thus our family had two funerals within two months. Villagers said that it was now my mother's turn to be bedridden.

"Before long, my sister married and left home, while my brother went from school into military service as a cadet. Mother, who was all by herself now, completely forgot to rest, and worked frantically to keep the farm and household going.

"When I want to scream from the pressure of having taken on too much work, or when I feel like complaining, or get angry that things don't go my way, I always think of my mother and how hard things were for her. There is no way I can compare to her. I constantly reprimand myself: Always try to appreciate things as they are. Don't complain! Don't get angry! Do your best!

"I can't remember much about life with my mother; nevertheless, the little that I do remember has been a great support for me and has spurred me on to do more. If we had lived together for ten or twenty years, her influence would probably have been even stronger."

Parents' thoughts, words, and deeds; their moments of joy and sadness; what they say to each other; the emotional ups and downs between them: all these are faithfully engraved in a child's soft and impressionable heart as words and images that can never be altered or erased. Children are formed by all of these influences. Regardless of whether children accept or reject them, in all probability they will grow up into living reflections of their parents and raise children of their own. Thus, all that is said, done, laughed at, resented, or cried over is preserved, with nothing altered. I feel how awesome it is to be a parent, and what a serious responsibility it is.

Mother seemed to recite the sutras in everything she did—reciting them with her body, so to speak, like Bodhidharma's teacher Hannyatara. I read about Hannyatara in a collection of Zen koans with a commentary called the *Shoyo-roku* (The Book of Equanimity). A certain king in eastern India, it says, invited Hannyatara to a feast to make him an offering of food. When a priest received such an offering, he would usually give a sermon or chant a sutra as a return gift to the Dharma. But Hannyatara ate and did nothing. The dissatisfied king asked, ''Why do you not recite a sutra?'' Hannyatara replied, ''Inhaling, exhaling, raising my leg or lowering it—my living form, the way I am, embodies the infinite Way of heaven and earth, the essence of a true sutra. What I am constantly doing is reciting the true and impeccable sutras, myriads of volumes' worth.''

In this limited lifetime, reciting the eternally true sutras with our imperfect, ordinary bodies, we follow the Way of heaven and earth. It is splendid if one can live this joy. How wonderful it is to be able to express one's own sutra or to read the sutra expressed by another. Not only human beings do it, but also plants and animals; and even rocks and water, which seem nonsentient. All preach the Law.

A renowned Japanese agricultural philosopher,

Ninomiya Sontoku (1787–1856), wrote, "Without sound, without smell, both heaven and earth continually repeat unwritten sutras." And Zen Master Dogen wrote, "All the colors of the mountain peaks, all the echoes of the valleys, are the form and voice of Shakyamuni Buddha." The Chinese Zen master Ta-chih (720–814) wrote, "All nonsentient beings expound the Buddha's teachings; all sentient beings listen." All basically say the same thing. What matters is whether the hearer is ready to hear.

A Parent's Last Words

What are the last words left to posterity by a dying parent? What is the "sutra" of the parent's life, written according to the way he or she lived, which remains to those left behind?

Is it not the message "You, too, will die someday"? In the words of Yoshio Toi, "to be alive is to embrace a dying life." A living thing cannot escape dying once. But no one knows when death will come. How should we live so that we can accept death whenever it comes? It is too late to think about it when it arrives. When we hear of someone's death, we compare the dead person's situation with ours and think seriously about the best way to live. It is only when funerals help us reflect on our own lives that they have meaning for us. And is not the devotion of our living selves the truest offering to the dead? Zen Master Dogen gives us a suggestion in his *Shobo-genzo* (Treasury of the True Dharma Eye). He says that all Zen Buddhists benefit by the example of religious discipline set by the founders of their sects, who died centuries ago. The best way to repay them for that benefit, he says, is to persevere in our day-to-day religious discipline.

The best offering to the departed is for us, those left behind, to live meaningful lives so that they need not worry about us and can continue tranquilly on their journey in the afterlife or peacefully attain buddhahood. Only when we lead meaningful lives do we comprehend the sutra of a parent, or the last words they wrote through the way they lived.

The World of Mutual Sympathy

One day King Pasenadi of Kosala climbed to the upper terrace of his palace with his queen, Mallika. The king, gazing out over the bustling streets and the vast mountains and plains of Kosala, turned to her and asked, "Mallika, is there someone in this great world that you love more than yourself?" After thinking awhile, she replied as though making a confession, "Your Majesty, I do not love anyone in this world as much as I love myself. And you, my lord?"

"Mallika, I cannot help but think the same."

They agreed with each other, but somehow they

felt this conclusion could not be in accord with the teachings of the Buddha, in whom they had taken refuge. The king and queen went to visit the Buddha in Jetavana Monastery. They told him what they had been thinking and then asked to be instructed. The Buddha, who had listened intently to them, nodded deeply and then replied in verse:

> The whole wide world we traverse with
>   our thoughts,
> And nothing that man finds is more dear
>   than self.
> Since, oh, so dear, the self to others is,
> Those who know the love of self
> Must harm no other man.
>
> (Samyutta-nikaya, pt 1, ch. 3)

Here is the prayer of the person who has no illusions, who has examined his own true nature. People often say "I don't care about my life as long as you are all right"; or "I will devote myself to the world, to humanity"; or "For my child I would go through fire and water." We must not overlook what lies in the shadows: the greedy self, secretly elated, going round and round calculating how to turn a situation to personal advantage. No matter what we do, we cannot eliminate human greed, what can be called instinctive self-love. It was this very condition that the Buddha saw clearly and that made him say "Harm no other man." Everyone loves himself or herself as much as I love myself. Just as I am wounded and suffering from heartless words and acts, other people are hurting and suffering. Just as I earnestly seek happiness, others also want to be happy. Therefore, do not hurt people. Do not make them suffer. Let us bring people happiness. Thus, in the highest sense self-love becomes love for others. Then it is ultimate self-love.

Consequently, those who cannot really love themselves fail to love others. Nowadays some people might kill someone just as they would kill an insect, simply because that person bothers them. It follows that they treat their own lives with the very same contempt.

When we achieve ultimate self-love, then, for the first time, the boundary between self and others naturally disappears, and others' joys and sorrows truly become one's own. When one sees someone suffering from an illness or from the problems of life, one cannot bear to look on doing nothing. One hastens to take care of the person or to find an immediate solution to his suffering. There is absolutely no thought of doing him a favor. One cannot help but do it as though it were for oneself. This is the realm of the oneness of the self and other. The Buddha gave it the name *ahimsa*, which was taught as the first of the five basic precepts: do not kill, do not steal, do not indulge in perverse sexual activity, do not lie, and do not drink to excess. Self-love, born of the undeniable human condition, is the starting point for the love of others. No, love of self and love of the other is the same love. This is a love that never wavers no matter what may happen. It is called compassion in Buddhism.

In Buddhism, the word love refers mainly to sexual desire, stemming from worldly passions. As a rule, when referring to Buddhist love, the term compassion is used. It means both shared suffering and tender affection. Shared suffering is ultimate self-love. When the final obstacle to self-love falls away as if the bottom has fallen out of one's own pail, one shares in another's joys and sorrows as if they were one's own. The literary critic Katsuichiro Kamei (1907–66) said that the smiles of many Buddha images were "the smiles that precede lamentation." The Buddha, taking on all of the sorrows and sufferings of living beings as his own, laments eternally. I believe it was his infinite compassion that gave expression to his loving smile.

One day when I visited Nara I was struck by a wooden statue of the great Chinese monk Chienchen, who for eleven years tried unsuccessfully to come to teach in Japan and was blind when he finally arrived in 754. At first glance the face looked sorrowful, but on further examination it seemed to be smiling. The haiku poet Basho (1644–94) wrote, "With a young leaf, I'd like to wipe the tears from your eyes." As I stood in front of the statue I felt the truth of these words. I have no idea how long I stood there. No one else was around. I felt outside time and space, as if only the statue and I existed, in communion. I felt I could sense what is called "the Buddha's compassion."

I have heard that the life of the Buddhist monk and poet Ryokan (1758–1831) was compassion itself. Whether weeping as he listened to the woes of a harlot or engrossed in playing with children, he had no trace of self-consciousness. Should the slightest awareness of *"I'm* playing" or *"I'm* listening" arise, at that moment it ceases to be compassion; it is not the love of the Buddha. I would like to continue to ask myself what the Buddha's love is and how we should live.

My Turning Point

My father died when he was fifty-two and I was seven. Now I am fifty-six. When I was about to turn fifty-two, I thought more and more about him. When he was near death, he called me to him and said in a tearful voice, "Since I have spent most of my life as an invalid, I was not able to do meaningful religious practice. My life is coming to an end without my being able to do the things I have wanted to do. Become a nun and do my part of the practice as well." Even now I vividly recall his voice. At age seven, having little idea what becoming a nun entailed, or what religious practice meant, I just cried out from the bottom of my heart, "I will become a nun! And as a nun I will do Daddy's part, too!"

By then I had been a novice for two years at Muryo-ji in the Japan Alps, where my aunt was the chief priest. I entered the temple at the age of five, my family having promised while I was still in my mother's womb that I would be sent there as a novice. My grandfather, who died fifteen years before I was born, was a leader of Shugendo—an eclectic form of Buddhism that stresses ascetic practice. Since my father was physically weak, he had had few children. My parents were surprised and pleased then, when they were blessed with my birth in their forties. At that time there was a prophecy from the spirit of my grandfather that I would enter the priesthood. And just when I was born came another prophecy, that I would enter a temple in the Japan Alps. When my aunt, the nun Shuzan, heard this, she was overcome with joy. She came for me when I was five.

My mother carried out all the household responsibilities alone while caring for my father, who had collapsed from illness in his mid-thirties. How must she have felt to have to give up her youngest child, even if it had been decreed by an oracle? After I left home at the age of five, my mother cried secretly for a year. Then, the next year on my birthday, January 15, she was unable to contain herself any longer. She came all the way to the temple on the pretext of bringing me a birthday present. Perhaps Shuzan could not bear looking at her forlorn figure. She said to me, "Go and hug your mother," but I would not. I merely went off and played. My mother remembered that incident till the day she died, at the the age of eighty. She said once, "If you had been a kitten or a puppy, I would have liked to put a string around your neck and taken you home. But when I saw that you made not the least move to follow me, the real truth of the situation dawned on me, right to the bottom of my heart: I had actually given you to the Buddha." Even so, I saw that she was crying as she recalled that.

For the child with whom she had spent so little time, my mother raised silkworms, spun the thread, wove the cloth, and made all the clothing I would need for the rest of my life, including the ceremonial robes, surplices, kimonos, and even obi sashes for kimonos. Clad in the embrace of the handwoven garments my mother made so devotedly with fervent prayer, I have earnestly followed the Buddha Way for fifty-one years, since I entered the temple at the age of five.

I was able to enter the great Way, open to me from the beginning, and to walk that path this far. Few of the many seekers of the Way have easily found it. When I look at my own life, I feel happy that the hopes and prayers and help of my parents, grandparents, and the many ancestors before them came together in this one living body of mine. Thus I feel very strongly that I must never neglect my religious faith, which is a gift from the Buddha. While praying that I may be allowed to live single-mindedly according to the Buddha's teachings, these days I find myself asking "Is this enough, Father? Have I managed to do your part as well?"

Throw Everything Away

In Nagoya as I left the newly built main hall of a branch temple of Eihei-ji and went around to the back, I came upon a cottage that seemed removed from the dust of the world. From it there unexpectedly resounded an earth-shakingly deep and vibrant voice beginning to chant a sutra. Startled, I stepped through the bush clover and wild chrysanthemums and hastily entered the small building. It was Sunday, November 9, 1968, the beginning of the monthly zazen gathering in Zen Master Ryoun Obora's dwelling, which was just a single room. The master was ninety-six years old. His bedding was usually left out, but today it was neatly put away, and he was wearing his religious robes and sitting at a *kotatsu*—a quilt-covered table with a heater under it. A long time ago he had taught at several universities and had been abbot of Aichi Semmon Niso-do (a training temple for female Soto Zen priests), before women could hold that post. It was hard to imagine that he had once been a remarkably tall and robust Zen master. A group of men and women in their late forties and fifties sat in a circle around him, their palms together in prayer. They apparently had long continued to attend his lectures even after his retirement. An old and well-used copy of *Fukan Zazengi* (Rules for Zazen) lay open in front of each of them.

He said, "People often ask, 'What is the meaning of zazen?' Many people answer that it is to become a buddha. But Zen Master Dogen said, 'Never intend to become a buddha. Zazen is not something to study.' The word *study* anticipates results. The zazen of Zen Master Dogen is not of the kind that anticipates the attainment of buddhahood or enlightenment. It is not such a give-and-take, grasping, beggarly zazen. What about your zazen? You may have been sitting in zazen for twenty or thirty years, but hasn't it been with the goal of gaining something? I'd like to hear your answers.''

At this point the master stopped speaking and his eyes opened wide and flashed around the room. How big and frightful he appeared, like a statue of a demonic guardian beside the gate to a Buddhist temple. The zazen practitioners dropped their eyes and shrank back like small animals under the glare of a lion. He continued: ''The zazen of Zen Master Dogen is zazen that throws out grasping, beggarly zazen. His is the zazen that seeks nothing and determines to throw everything away.''

How expressive his face was as he repeated the gesture of throwing something away with his big hands, laughing good-naturedly. ''If you just throw it all away and don't go looking for something, at that point your own easy entrance into the Way will be manifested. That is Zen Master Dogen's zazen.''

Such a beautiful, smiling face made me recall many things from twenty years earlier. At that time I was in a training temple. When I visited a temple called Hoan-den Gokoku-in, still surrounded by the rubble of war, Ryoun Obora appeared from behind a shanty wearing a tattered robe. At first glance, I mistook him for a servant monk. His beautiful, smiling face also reminded me of his flat refusal, despite strong recommendations, to become chief priest at the head temple. As I remembered all this, I was brought face to face with the immense power of his injunction to throw everything away.

He had such vitality that it was hard to believe he was ninety-six years old. He continued his lecture, "Zazen Is Not Study," for close to two hours. I recognized the beauty and superhuman power of someone living according to his Buddhist vows. When I asked him the secret of his long life, he replied, "So far I have never gone without three meals a day. That is all. It seems like nothing, but it is actually not such an easy thing to do, and it has deep meaning." When I asked him if he could give me an easier explanation, he went on, "That is something to be delved into depending on the listener's capacity." This was all the more a koan. Come to think of it, we often skip meals for various reasons. In Zen practice, breakfast is called *gyoshuku,* meaning "practicing the way of rice gruel," just as lunch is *gyohatsu,* meaning "practicing the way of the bowls." We practice the gruel; we practice the bowls. Meals are zazen; meals are religious practice. We tend to forget this, so that they become a mundane matter of what we want or do not want. Or our usual attitude might be that we just eat to feed ourselves. With that attitude we cannot possibly eat properly, and what is not eaten properly will not nourish the body and mind. What a splendid thing that for almost ninety-seven years the master had taken his daily meals without ever missing one.

Just as I was thinking that a long visit would tire him and that I should think of leaving, he deliberately straightened up and said in a voice loud enough to make the room shake: "Zen Master Dogen was great because he kept his distance from fame and profit. When the retired emperor Go-saga [1220–72] offered him the most prestigious kind of Buddhist monk's robe, dyed purple and bestowed only by emperors, Master Dogen refused it three times. When at last he was obliged to accept it, he composed this verse:

> Though the valley of Eihei-ji is shallow,
> Grave is the edict of the emperor.
> If an old man were to wear a purple robe,
> He would be laughed at
>   by monkeys and cranes.

He kept the robe in a place of honor at Eihei-ji and never wore it. There are too many priests nowadays trading on the name of Buddhism for fame and fortune. It is an inexcusable thing to the buddhas and the patriarchs. I am too old to do anything more. I have to ask all you young people to help out. Please tell those who have mistaken the Way that the value of Buddhism has nothing to do with fame and fortune and that herein lies the true way of living.'' His voice had become a lamentation, painful even to hear, against the religious world and modern society.

I received this request of his with deep emotion and resolve. He gave me a plaque on which he had written a single Chinese character meaning ''circle,'' that is, ''perfect.'' I prayed in my heart for his health, then hurried back in the late afternoon along the dusty road to our training temple.

About a month later he died.

There is one more thing about him that I cannot forget. It was in the spring of my third year as a nun, when I was eighteen and in practice at a training temple. I had gone for one week to a temple connected with Zen Master Taishun Sato to help with the precepts ceremony. Occasionally, Zen Master Obora would take the place of Zen Master Sato in giving sermons or heading the *shosan,* in the precepts ceremony. In the *shosan* interview, practicing monks and nuns publicly question the master on points of Buddhist doctrine. We helpers were also given a turn to pose questions. Originally, the *shosan* was meant to be a lively, heated question-and-answer session, but it had just become a ritual that contributed to the atmosphere of the precepts ceremony. Furthermore, the practicing monks and nuns scheduled to take part in the *shosan* had been told that, because the master was old and tired, they would be allowed to ask only one question each.

At last the *shosan* began, and in high spirits all the others raised their voices in the great Buddha Hall, asking their commonplace questions about the Way. I decided to ask a question about the meaning of life and death, which had sorely perplexed me. As I stood there in my perplexity in the great Buddha Hall full of ordained monks and nuns, and lay persons, where there was hardly room to stand, I felt as if I were lost deep in the mountains. I felt that the only way out was to fling myself before Zen Master Obora, as an earth-bound creature who was completely lost in matters of life and death or delusion and enlightenment.

I put my question implicitly by quoting from a poem by Zen Master Dogen:

Life and death are to be loved,
Changing like the fleeting clouds.
Walking either the path of delusion
    or enlightenment
Is only walking in a dream.

In the silence that had awaited Zen Master Obora's response, his quiet voice could be heard throughout the hall. He countered my question with another: "What does it mean to say 'Life and death, as they are, is nirvana'?"

The question was over my head. Since I could not think of an answer, I stood mute with my head bowed. Then he said, "Practice for thirty years and then come back; then ask me again.'' With these severe words of encouragement, I returned to my place.

Taking up the challenge to understand that ''life and death, as they are, is nirvana,'' I silently vowed to practice the Way and listen to the Buddha's teachings and then meet Zen Master Obora again. At the same time, I figured out exactly how old he would be in thirty years. At that time he was seventy-eight. In thirty years he would be one hundred and eight. Thirty years is a long time in a life, and it concerned me to think of his advanced age.

In no time, eighteen years had passed. Fortunately he was blessed with longevity and was now ninety-six. I continued to have the good fortune of coming every month to teach over the past six or seven years at the temple, where I had trained, close to Zen Master Obora's dwelling. Now, finally, I could at least nod in agreement with the description in the ''Life and Death'' section of the *Shobo-genzo,* but to try and grasp the deepest significance of ''Life and death, as they are, is nirvana'' gave me the hopeless feeling of trying to scratch the sole of my foot through the bottom of my shoe. Although I continued to regret my lack of understanding each time I met him, in the end those words became his last will and testament to me.

I sat before his memorial tablet and thought deeply. I decided that my offering would be a vow to live by the maxim "Life and death, as they are, is nirvana."

Zazen That Amounts to Nothing

On February 29, 1966, I arrived in Kyoto at dusk. It was raining. I was wearing worn-out wooden clogs and did not have an umbrella with me, so I considered taking a taxi to the temple, where I would be attending a *sesshin* to engage in intense zazen meditation. I did not know exactly where the temple was, let alone how to get there on my own. Feeling, however, that it was essential not to indulge myself before a *sesshin*, I set off by bus, determined to find my way.

After what seemed a couple of hours, I finally arrived at Shaka-taniguchi, where the temple was located. Except for a single street light at the bus stop, everything was pitch black. In the pouring rain, the mountains and houses were submerged in dark shadows. I asked a young girl who had gotten off the bus with me if she knew where the temple called Antai-ji was, and she pointed to a thicket straight ahead. Lifting the hems of my nun's robes, I ran toward it in the rain. Stumbling over rocks on the mountain path leading to the temple, I pushed my way through the thicket and came to what seemed to be the entrance.

Was it Antai-ji or not? I was still unsure. But by peering intently in the faint light that came from within, I was able to read the words "Antai-ji, the

Purple Bamboo Grove Monastery'' carved into a large, timeworn board. Thinking I had arrived at last, I pushed open the heavy outer door and called out, but no one answered. There seemed to be people moving about in the next room. I considered opening the inner door, but first tried asking for help from the outside. It was lucky that I did not open that door—that was where the trainee monks were bathing. A voice answered my call: "Please hit the board twice."

Where was it? There was not a single light in that spacious entrance hall. By groping about, I was able to locate the board and hit it twice, as I had been instructed. The board was so worn that it had a large concave area in the center—it made a funny, hollow sound. Before long a trainee monk appeared, and then Zen Master Kosho Uchiyama came out to greet me: "How good of you to come, Reverend Aoyama! Please remove your outer robe and make yourself comfortable." His welcome, which did away with formalities, made me feel relieved at finally having reached my destination. I visited his quarters right away to receive instructions concerning the *sesshin*.

On the first day of March, I awoke to the ringing of the temple bell at 4 A.M. I hurried over the long, creaky corridors toward the meditation hall. The cold wind blowing up through the cracks in the floorboards cut at my bare feet.

"Meditation hall" sounds impressive, but at Antai-ji it was just a single dilapidated room with only fifteen tatami mats on a low platform. At its entrance these words of instruction were posted: "Leave others alone. Individuals must engage in their own spiritual practice"; and "Everything must be done in silence. There must be no audible sutra reading or greetings." The night before, Zen Master Uchiyama had said, "Chanting the sutras would spoil our concentration, interrupting our zazen practice. *Sesshin* here means sitting in meditation for five days as though it were a single sitting."

All the participants entered the meditation hall and began to meditate in silence. The paper curtain in front of the entrance was lowered, and the signal to begin zazen was given. In this way, the five-day *sesshin* commenced without ceremony.

The hall was bitter cold. Icy drafts entered it from all directions, even blowing under my robes. Clumsy paper curtains that appeared to be made of sheets of wrapping paper from parcels covered the inside walls, flapping noisily in the drafts.

There was a five-minute break known as *chukai* every hour. It was during one of these breaks that I whispered to another woman in the restroom, "Cold, isn't it!" She whispered back, "It's comfortable now. Last month, there weren't any curtains, so the snow fell right on our heads."

I came down with a cold on the third day. I thought it would be a shame to stop meditating because of a cold. After all, I had wanted to participate in this *sesshin* for a long time. Since I wanted to get over my cold as soon as possible and stop bothering the people around me with my sneezing and coughing, I bundled up in as many layers of clothing as I could, including my night clothes, to try to sweat out my cold.

Zen Master Uchiyama worried about me and gave me some medicine, and so did the nun working in the kitchen. At night they put a foot-warmer in my bedding. I felt grateful—it was more than I deserved—and sorry, since I believed that my cold was due to my own carelessness. I continued in this way and was able to complete the *sesshin* without missing even a single sitting.

I had a bit of trouble at mealtimes, however. The master and monks seemed to finish very quickly, but perhaps this was the regular pace at monasteries. There was no sign of haste in the way they ate, yet they each consumed two bowls of rice. I had been one of the faster eaters at the training temple where I lived, but here I was no match at all. In addition, the meals included brown rice. Since this was the first time I had eaten it, I mistook it for *sakura-meshi* (rice cooked in sake and soy sauce), a favorite dish of mine, and was secretly delighted when it was scooped into my bowl. But when I took a good look at it, I noticed that it was actually brown rice. Hesitantly, I put some in my mouth. It had been skillfully prepared, but it was harder than white rice and smelled of bran. There were even a few unhulled grains in my bowl.

Looking around me, I saw that no one was trying to pick out the unhulled grains, but that everyone was eating with gusto, so I tried to do the same. Two orange slices with rinds had been placed on top of the salad, and these, too, were being devoured, rinds and all. It being Zen vegetarian cooking, the only meaty things were the small dried sardines in the bean-paste soup. Though the others finished effortlessly in time for a second serving, my first serving of brown rice seemed not to diminish no matter how much I ate, perhaps because the trainee monk had packed my bowl so well. Bewildered, I swallowed the coarse brown rice, ate the orange slices, rinds and all, the dried sardines, heads and all, and ended up being one of the last to put down my chopsticks, along with a student who looked like a beginner.

While I was eating, I thought about the time the Buddhist priest and scholar Kazuyoshi Kino invited me over to try brown rice. I was afraid that I would have stomach trouble, so I declined. I now realized that I should have accepted his invitation. I recalled his words: "If there is a task that you must do, no matter how much you detest doing it, you must do it thinking 'I love it, I love it.'" There was nothing to keep me from enjoying the brown rice that everyone else was eating with relish. I told myself that I must somehow get to like it during the five days of the *sesshin*.

Before meals we did not chant the sutras as usual, nor did we perform the ritual of removing the cloth covers around our bowls as is customary at other temples. Still, every part of the day was strictly regulated. The foreigners and other beginners were not yet familiar with the temple routine and were apt to forget that silence was to be observed. Sometimes they were noisy. Had I been in charge, I would have told them to be quiet, but Zen Master Uchiyama and the trainee monks pretended not to notice. Later, Zen Master Uchiyama explained, "Not saying anything at such times is also part of one's spiritual practice. You are tempted to say 'Be quiet!' but should you do so, that would be the end of it. People would merely be obsessed with being quiet. If zazen is truly practiced, it naturally happens that no sounds are made. Until this comes about, you must guide people kindly in their zazen."

No regular cleaning was done during the *sesshin*. The trainee monks had simplified everything as much as possible so that the participants could devote themselves exclusively to zazen. They could not very well go without cleaning at all for five days, but they managed to restrict it to less than twenty minutes during the break after breakfast. They would fill buckets with water and carry them silently to the temple. Anyone who comes to An-tai-ji is treated as a trainee, regardless of whether he is a university professor or a company president. Each person was expected to help clean the floor. People would tuck up their clothing and, without a word, wipe the floor with a wet cloth at lightning speed; then they would quickly enter the meditation hall.

The signal to begin zazen was then given. No matter how many hours pass, no matter whether dusk falls, dawn comes, or whole days go by,

everyone sits like a simpleton in a speechless
world. There are no lectures by the master, no
chanting of sutras, no circulating of the *kyosaku*
(the meditation stick used to awaken those who
doze), and no interviews between the master and
disciples. There is not a single thing to distract
one; there is no one to show off to. Left alone by
the monk in charge, everyone faces the wall from
beginning to end. The meditation stick yawns
upon the sutra table. No matter how much you
doze, there is no one there to do you the favor of
waking you.

Yet it is impossible to sleep for five days. Your
eyes open even though you may not want them to,
and you must come face to face with yourself. For
the first time, I came to know real zazen, in which
people must be led with true kindness. After all,
living is neither something that other people can
help you do nor something that you can have them
do in your place. You are completely on your own.
You sit in a state of awareness, straightening your
back and confronting that fact. Zazen as practiced
at Antai-ji is the true way human beings should
live. It is ideal zazen.

The other day I heard the story of a person who
had been beaten for a week at a Zen temple
known for its cruelty. He proudly boasted about
such things as being awakened at three in the
morning, being struck again and again, how his
shoulders became swollen, and how meditation
sticks would break while being used to beat the
trainees. He related that if he so much as moved a

muscle he would be reprimanded so loudly that it would make him start. He also described the last meal at the week's end, when an elderly kitchen supervisor was brought before the participants and made to bow deeply and apologize for not having correctly prepared the miso soup throughout the week.

That is a disgusting way of leading zazen. It is intolerable that an exceedingly large number of both monks and lay people understand such severe methods to be true zazen practice. If a lay person is aroused at two or three in the morning, if the meditation stick breaks on his shoulder, and if he is yelled at in a voice loud enough to make him start, this practice would naturally seem harsh to him. But it is really the easier way of practicing zazen. Try being left alone, regardless of whether day breaks or night falls. You start to want to scream "Hit me!" or "Say something!" Left all alone, a person cannot stand himself. Even if you were to cry out, it would be useless. Such is life. The more we struggle, the muddier the water becomes. There is no one to save us; no one to breathe for us; no one to get sick in our place. We must live our own lives. Thus we must do zazen with determination.

For over thirty years the Chinese Zen master Ta-mei Fa-ch'ang secluded himself deep in the mountains and practiced zazen. He spent his life seeing the mountains turn green in the spring and red in the autumn, and did not even try to count the passing months and years. People of long ago

practiced zazen in that manner. We who are weak
and fragile cannot practice in that way. Instead,
we gather in a single hall and are kindly placed in
a situation where we can meditate as if we were sitting alone under the trees or on the rocks in an
isolated mountain valley. Such is the zazen practiced at Antai-ji. That is truly the kind way to
lead a *sesshin*.

The five-day *sesshin* ended with a number of
rituals. The paper curtains at the entrance to the
meditation hall were raised, and everyone pro-
ceeded from the hall to the master's quarters.
There we all bowed deeply and thanked him from
the bottom of our hearts. Continuing on, we went
to the kitchen and bowed in gratitude to the old
nun in charge of the meals. These rituals, in which
a dynamic spirit was manifested in form, spontaneously unfolded one after the other. For a person
like me who was used to empty religious practice,
everything in these rituals was revealing, down to
the most insignificant detail. It was then that I
recognized the original purpose of those solemn
rituals. The first words we uttered after the five
days of silence were "Thank you very much."
These words after the long silence gave me a new
understanding of the value of speech.

Before long, the wooden clappers signaled
teatime. For the first time, I took a close look at the
people with whom I had meditated for five days
and was surprised to find that almost half of them
were foreigners. I learned that most of them had
saved for three or four years to come to Japan in

search of Zen. After visiting various Zen training halls, they had settled on this temple, secured temporary lodgings nearby, and commuted to the monthly *sesshin,* zazen sessions, and lectures on Zen. For example, the couple who happened to sit next to me took turns: from four in the morning until noon, the wife was there; from noon until bedtime, the husband. When I asked why they did this, they replied, "Since we have a baby, we can't both be away from home at the same time." They seemed truly dedicated to Zen.

Other participants came all the way from Kyushu, Shikoku, Niigata, and Tokyo. Furthermore, they did so every month. I was amazed to find that I, who thought I had come from far away, was among those who lived closest. The Japanese participants all felt that they could not compare in zeal with the foreigners, who had left everything behind to come to Japan. I thought that I had understood that distance is not a problem for the mind that seeks the Dharma, but these people provided me with new insights into that truth.

Zen Master Uchiyama had said the previous fall, "If a person has the mind that seeks, he or she should come to Antai-ji." I now understood in my heart that this was not an exaggeration but was in fact happening. We often make excuses for not being able to take part in zazen sessions and Zen lectures, saying that we are too busy or that the place is too far away. These are lame excuses. If you really have a mind that seeks, you can find time for these activities. People who say they do not have the time lack willpower.

Smiling wryly, Zen Master Uchiyama said, "Even though so many foreigners come here, not a single trainee monk at this temple can speak English. On top of this, my Japanese is not standard. It is a Tokyo dialect, so that some of the words and expressions I use are not in the dictionary. Thus the foreigners have a hard time understanding me."

Yet foreigners gather in great numbers at Antai-ji. A foreign woman who had, together with myself, spent five days living and meditating at the temple, said in broken Japanese that the zazen of the Soto Zen sect was more difficult than that of the Rinzai Zen sect. She said that this was because sitting itself was a koan for Soto Zen. Even though the foreigners did not understand Zen Master Uchiyama's every word, they seemed to grasp exactly what was essential. After all, it is not important to understand something with words or with the intellect.

There was a student having a hard time because of pain in his legs from sitting for long periods in meditation. He appeared to be new to zazen. No one thought he would last through the *sesshin*. In spite of that, he persevered to the end. Turning to him, Master Uchiyama said with a teasing smile, "You are great. You are worthy of an award for your fighting spirit. You would be all right even if you were in jail." (Prisoners in Japan sit on the floor.) Then to everyone he said, "The zazen prac-

ticed here amounts to nothing, no matter how long
you sit. But it would come in handy were you to be
put in jail," and he laughed. Zazen is a world in
which we have thrown away all of the cravings of
the mind, including all forms of seeking and anticipation. Zazen is a world beyond losses and
gains—even beyond seeking enlightenment. One
simply sits, casting off the whole of one's beggarly
disposition. That is what Zen Master Uchiyama
calls "the zazen that amounts to nothing."

Serving Others as a Bridge

One day while perusing the analects of T'ang
dynasty Zen monks, I was struck by the lines
"Helping donkeys to cross and horses to cross."
Even nuns in training sometimes lose sight of the
right course. So many different kinds of people are
nuns. To be a bridge on which all these believers
could somehow cross to the Other Shore of enlightenment is my work. Those lines taught me
my vocation, and I have taken them to heart.

Later when I heard that Emperor Showa had assigned "bridge" as the theme for the New Year's
poetry party at the Imperial Palace, those lines
again came to mind. I was not invited to the party,
but I wrote a poem on the theme, incorporating
those lines:

Helping donkeys to cross
And horses to cross:

Such a bridge I wish to be,
Yet I am merely helped to cross.

During the T'ang dynasty in China, there was a great Zen master named Chao-chou. To reach his temple it was necessary to cross what had become known as Chao-chou's bridge. A monk once asked him, "What is your bridge?" He did not mean the bridge on the way to the temple, but Chao-chou's practice of Buddhism. Chao-chou answered, "It helps both donkeys and horses to cross."

A bridge allows not only donkeys to cross it, but more valuable animals like horses. A bridge does not distinguish between friends and enemies or saints and sinners. It unconditionally helps anyone to cross. It allows them over whatever their attitude is toward it, even if they kick at it or urinate on it. Few people cross it with gratitude. Chao-chou selflessly wished that all people might cross from This Shore of delusion to the Other Shore of enlightenment. His practice, like that of a great bodhisattva, is splendidly symbolized by a bridge.

What about me? What about my petty self that picks and chooses according to its own convenience? Do I think it is all right for the horse to cross over, but not the donkey? Is it all right for my friends but not my enemies? It is my ego that desires praise and makes me want to be appreciated as a bridge and thanked before helping someone to cross, and that cannot avoid imposing conditions on those who cross. It is also my ego that sulks, muttering that the person urinating on the bridge should not be helped to cross.

Ever focusing on the lines "Helping donkeys to cross / And horses to cross" as if I were repeatedly invoking Amida, I have spent my time meeting practitioners and believers. One day it suddenly occurred to me that simply being a bridge was not enough; one has to become a ferryman. People who are about to cross the bridge called Buddhism know that the Other Shore is a more splendid world than this mundane, deluded world. They also know that the way to reach it is by crossing that bridge.

Some people live in misery on This Shore without even knowing that the Other Shore exists. There are many people like this. There are also many others who know about the Other Shore but do not want to cross over, saying that This Shore is better. To let them know of the Other Shore, to have them see its splendor, and to awaken in them the desire to reach it, it is not enough simply to be a bridge. One must reach out. This is the role of the ferryman. In other words, one must be kind enough to remain for a while on This Shore with the desire to guide others toward salvation by helping them satisfy their present needs and desires, such as food, wealth, fame, and love. At the same time, one tries to draw them to a world beyond, of higher things. If one is a Buddhist monk or priest, one must throw aside one's robes and become involved in the world in order to weep, suffer, and laugh with other people. Gradually people will become aware of the true Way and be drawn toward it. Undertaking a vow and discipline to help people in that manner is symbolized by the thirty-three forms of Kannon.

It is written in the Kannon Sutra: "In the lands of the universe there is no place where [Kannon] is not manifested." Always and everywhere, the working of Kannon is revealed. If only we open our mind's eye, we find that the person we thought we disliked is actually a manifestation of Kannon in disguise, helping us to recognize our selfishness. Sickness, failure, and separation from those we love are the Buddha's means of showing us that we must end our self-indulgence, that we must awaken to the truth of life. We are surrounded by the Buddha's arrangements to help us.

Reflecting thus far, I realized that my thinking I was a bridge that helped anyone across was presumptuous. I saw that actually I, too, am being helped across.